MAYA
CIVILIZATION

S M I T H S O N I A N
EXPLORING THE ANCIENT WORLD
JEREMY A. SABLOFF, Editor

MAYA CIVILIZATION

By T. PATRICK CULBERT

St. Remy Press • Montreal

Smithsonian Books • Washington, D.C.

EXPLORING THE ANCIENT WORLD
was produced by
ST. REMY PRESS

Publisher	Kenneth Winchester
President	Pierre Léveillé
Managing Editor	Carolyn Jackson
Managing Art Director	Diane Denoncourt
Production Manager	Michelle Turbide
Administrator	Natalie Watanabe

Staff for *MAYA CIVILIZATION*

Editors	Michael Ballantyne
	Daniel McBain
Art Director	Chantal Bilodeau
Picture Editor	Christopher Jackson
Researcher	Olga Dzatko
Assistant Editor	Jennifer Meltzer
Photo Assistant	Geneviève Monette
Designer	Sara Grynspan
Illustrators	Maryse Doray
	Robert Paquet
	Maryo Proulx
Systems Coordinator	Jean-Luc Roy
Administrative Assistant	Dominique Gagné
Indexer	Christine Jacobs
Proofreader	Judy Yelon

THE SMITHSONIAN INSTITUTION

Secretary	Robert McC. Adams
Assistant Secretary for External Affairs	Thomas E. Lovejoy
Director, Smithsonian Institution Press	Felix C. Lowe

SMITHSONIAN BOOKS

Editor-in-Chief	Patricia Gallagher
Senior Editor	Alexis Doster III
Editors	Amy Donovan
	Joe Goodwin
Assistant Editors	Brian D. Kennedy
	Sonia Reece
Senior Picture Editor	Frances C. Rowsell
Picture Editors	Carrie F. Bruns
	R. Jenny Takacs
Picture Research	V. Susan Guardado
Production Editor	Patricia Upchurch
Business Manager	Stephen J. Bergstrom

Library of Congress Cataloging-in-Publication Data
Culbert, T. Patrick
  Maya Civilization / T. Patrick Culbert
    p. cm. — (Exploring the ancient world)
  Includes bibliographical references and index.
  ISBN 0-89599-036-9
  1. Mayas—Antiquities. 2. Mexico—Antiquities. 3. Central America—
    Antiquities I. Title.   II. Series.
F1435.C83   1993
972'.01—dc20   93-32306
                                                  CIP

Manufactured and printed in Canada.
First Edition

10 9 8 7 6 5 4 3 2 1

FRONT COVER PHOTO: *In A.D. 731, this proud ruler was portrayed on a stela at the site of Arroyo de Piedra. In the monument's text, however, he names himself a vassal of the king of nearby Dos Pilas.*

BACK COVER PHOTO: *Temple of the Inscriptions, Palenque, Mexico.*

CONTENTS

EDITOR'S FOREWORD

If the spate of recent books on the subject, front-page articles in national newspapers and magazines on newly discovered royal tombs, and dozens of active field projects are reliable clues, then it is reasonable to assume that the ancient Maya are exceedingly popular. If there is still any doubt, the multitudes of tourists visiting archaeological sites in Mexico, Belize, Guatemala, and Honduras, and the bulging college classrooms for Maya courses should be evidence enough of the interest in both the public and scholarly arenas.

One of the reasons for all this interest in the ancient Maya is that scholarly understanding of their fascinating civilization has grown by leaps and bounds in recent years as traditional views of the Maya have been shown to be wrong. The field of Maya archaeology is thus in a state of flux as a new model of the complex social, economic, political, and religious organization of Maya civilization is just beginning to emerge. There is considerable excitement in the scholarly community about the Maya. It seems that each month—if not week or day—brings reports of new information that broadens our knowledge of the Maya and enhances our insights into the functioning of Maya civilization and how it developed through time.

This book fits in perfectly with the goals of the *Exploring the Ancient World* series by placing the ongoing changes in thinking about the ancient Maya in a historical context and then offering readers a state-of-the-art overview of current archaeological conceptions of the development of Classic Maya civilization and its ultimate demise. Professor T. Patrick Culbert explains that the traditional view—a Classic Maya society that lived in isolation in its jungle setting, with small, peaceful, non-urban ceremonial centers, extensive agriculture, and esoteric hieroglyphic writing—has been shown in recent years to be untenable. In clear, understandable prose, Professor Culbert presents new insights into the tropical rainforest environment, demography, and agriculture of the Classic Maya, and shows how these new data, when coupled with the major advances in the decipherment of Maya writing, have led to a new model of Maya civilization.

This new model, which Professor Culbert examines in the pages that follow, emphasizes the urban nature of Maya centers, the intensive agricultural systems that supported these cities, and the competition and warfare that characterized the relation among the cities. In describing the new model, he is able to dispel the old aura of mystery that surrounded discussions of the ancient Maya and to indicate how the Classic civilization arose, thrived for many centuries, and finally collapsed.

Professor Culbert is a highly regarded authority on Maya civilization. He is an expert on Maya ceramics and the tropical environment and has published on a wide variety of topics in Maya archaeology. He is the author of *The Lost Civilization: The Story of the Classic Maya*, *The Ceramic History of the Central Highlands of Chiapas, Mexico*, and *Introducing Culture* (with E. Schusky), and is the editor of *The Classic Maya Collapse*, *Precolumbian Population History in the Maya Lowlands* (with D. Rice), and *Classic Maya Political History*. He received his doctorate from the University of Chicago, and is a Professor of Anthropology at the University of Arizona.

Professor Culbert's expertise will be clearly evident as he skillfully immerses readers in the excitement of research in the tropical lowlands and the optimistic vitality that now pervades the field of Maya archaeology.

Jeremy A. Sabloff,
University of Pittsburgh

Editors' note: We should, perhaps, explain the author's policy regarding accents. All words in Maya languages are accented on the last syllable. When writing in Spanish, many Maya words require accents. When writing in English, however, Professor Culbert considers it unnecessary (in fact, incorrect) to accent Maya words as though one were writing in Spanish.

In an aerial view, the site of Kabah, Yucatan, emerges from the surrounding forest. Early reports of mysterious cities hidden in the jungle civilizations that attracted scores of bold—and sometimes very eccentric—adventurers to Maya sites in the 1800s.

engendered romantic theories of lost

1

SETTING THE STAGE

From the moment of its discovery, Maya civilization has fueled the imaginations of those with a bent for romance. Giant stone temples, some as tall as 20-story buildings, lurk within a brooding, trackless forest. Ancient tombs contain royal riches—the handiwork of master artisans—and a long-undeciphered script holding centuries-old secrets. Adding to the intrigue is the realization that the creators of this flourishing culture disappeared, leaving a vast area empty and lifeless. Once-majestic pyramids returned to the forest from which they had sprung. For more than a century, charlatans, madmen, and adventurers have trooped through the Central American jungle, eventually returning home to pack lecture halls or to write books for a curious public.

These purveyors of dreams and fantasies have recounted unlikely adventures, often telling of discoveries that, no sooner reported, mysteriously vanished. Some enthusiasts claimed the Maya had come from a lost Atlantis; others, that they had been instructed by ancient extraterrestrial astronauts. They reputedly had created remarkable technologies—now lost—or unearthed the philosophical keys to the universe. As the tales spun on, the Maya grew ever more enigmatic, their accomplishments increasingly fantastic.

Meanwhile, generations of archaeologists have labored to make sense of the Maya—and to replace fantasy with fact. True understanding of this puzzling culture has grown as discovery followed discovery. Frequently, though, as one riddle is solved, another is unveiled, providing scientists with genuine mysteries as fascinating as the fabrications of early pseudo-scholarly adventurers. A book like this can be no more than a progress report about the state of knowledge today. It is an exciting time for such a report, because ideas about the Maya have been completely transformed over the last 30 years or so; given the current pace of research, some of this book may even be passé before it is published.

One important change has been the dismantling of a mistaken, albeit quite appealing, image of ancient Maya civilization. Generated by archaeologists during the first half of the 20th century, this portrait idealizes the Maya as peaceable and gentle, rich in intellectual and artistic accomplishments—a people free of the vices tainting the rest of humankind. The Maya, of course, were not like this at all; but the dearth of real evidence about their civilization permitted as pastoral and noble a portrayal as one desired. The lingering misconception is amply evinced by romantic attempts to recreate the lifestyle of the ancient Maya. On a recent visit to the Maya lowlands, I met an expatriate New Zealander carving wood by the edge of a lake. He had fled the strain of a high-powered career and settled down in a place where, he claimed, untold generations had lived in harmony, both with the land and themselves. Although he himself had found peace in his adopted home, he was quite wrong about his spiritual ancestors, for the Maya had overpopulated and overexploited their environment, had fought each other viciously, and eventually had destroyed themselves. The New Zealander, not unlike scores of archaeologists and dreamers before him, had reinvented the Maya. He had created an imaginary people in order to fulfill a wish for peace and harmony.

But if recent knowledge has stripped the ancient Maya of their former romantic guise, have we rendered them dull, an early civilization like any other? Hardly. For Maya studies now seethe with energy and argument. New, exciting vistas are opening before us one after the other. Perhaps the most fascinating questions—certainly the most revolutionary—spring from the fact that the

The ancient Maya confirmed their beliefs in the gods through works such as this sculpture of the Young Maize God (c. 775) from Copan, Honduras. Maize was the most important food plant for the Maya and was, in their creation myths, the substance from which the gods fashioned the first humans.

The terraced, pyramidal Temples I and II close the east and west sides of the Great Plaza at Tikal, Guatemala. Temple I (in the background), also known as the Temple of the Giant Jaguar, soars 145 feet (44 meters) above what was the city. Ruler A, the first of the great Late Classic rulers of Tikal, was buried deep within it. Temple II, built slightly earlier than Temple I, may be the burial place of the principal wife of Ruler A, although her tomb has not yet been discovered.

Maya of the Classic period (A.D. 250-950) have suddenly been transformed from a prehistoric to an historic civilization. In a stunning breakthrough in 1960, the Maya hieroglyphic code was broken; since that date, half the Classic inscriptions have been deciphered. Now we can read of wars won and lost, the rise and fall of sites of power, the birth and death of kings. We catch glimpses of great, interwoven royal families and marvel at the political geniuses wheeling and dealing their way to power. Sometimes we can even gaze upon the skeletons of the once-great, and the treasures that accompanied them to the grave.

Other important questions still center on traditional archaeological data. Still in ferment, for example, is the issue of when and how Maya civilization began. Fanciful speculations about the ancestors of the Maya—that they were the Lost Tribes of Israel, the Phoenicians, or wandering refugees from Atlantis—have long been put to rest. So have the old anthropological suggestions that Maya civilization must have been imported whole from some more salubrious highland region, the rain forest being too enervating an environment to foster a civilization. (A whole generation of British novelists instructed us that rain forests inevitably reduced colonial civil servants to lethargy—if they didn't drive them to madness.) One by one, each of these ideas about an extraneous origin for Maya civilization was dispelled as large archaeological projects reached deeply buried levels, pushing the date for Maya civilization farther and farther into the past. It became clear that the civilization had indeed germinated in the same location where it later flourished. But only within the last few years has it been realized that the largest of all Maya sites, El Mirador, in the remote reaches of northern Guatemala, is earlier than all the more famous and more popular sites. Neighboring Nakbe, not so large but still with enormous temple-pyramids, is earlier yet. Why such large sites are the very earliest is one of the new puzzles Mayanists must solve.

Ideas about population density and food-production systems also are evolving rapidly. We have discarded earlier notions of a very small Maya population supported completely by a conservative, ecologically sound system of slash-and-burn farming. This conclusion was disproved by archaeological research demonstrating that Maya populations were staggeringly high—especially in the Late Classic period (A.D. 600-830)—and that the Maya were forced into a variety of intensive agricultural techniques. Now, debate centers on the success of Maya adaptation to environment; as the old agricultural area is rapidly recolonized by modern-day peasant farmers, this research may well have implications for future use of the forest and its resources.

Finally, there are still unresolved questions related to the fact that in the ninth century, the Maya in the southern half of the lowlands suffered a disastrous collapse. Their thriving civilization fell, and the majority of their population was lost. Given the population's original size, this phenomenon rates as one of the great demographic disasters in world history. What caused it? Were the Maya in some way responsible for their own demise, through, perhaps, social or ecological mismanagement? While in recent years we have come closer to answering these questions, our discoveries have exposed new puzzles—conundrums that remain unsolved.

These are some of the issues in Maya research today. The task of this book is to follow the progress of study as it traces the history of the Maya.

THE ARENA AND ITS PLAYERS

The ancient Maya—like their descendants today—spoke a group of closely related languages with roughly the same number of similarities and differences as those between the Romance languages of Europe. Today, 28 Maya languages are still spoken in Mexico and Central America. Except for the Huastecs—a Maya-speaking group now living on the northern gulf coast of Mexico—all the modern Maya languages occur in a single block that covers parts of southern Mexico, Guatemala, Belize, and sections of El Salvador and Honduras. This monolithic block, along with evidence that two of the Maya languages were written in hieroglyphic script a millennium ago, indicates that the Maya have inhabited the area since ancient times.

Most of the land occupied by the Maya is the low-lying Yucatan Peninsula, a limestone shelf that juts northward from the backbone of the continent into the Gulf of Mexico. While this plateau rose from the ocean long before the ancestors of the Maya first appeared, its formation is recent in geological time (a few million years ago). In these steamy tropical lowlands, the Maya erected

Mexico
Guatemala
Belize
El Salvador
Honduras

Isla Cerritos

Komchen
Dzibilchaltun
Izamal
Oxkintok   Mayapan   Chichen Itza
Uxmal   Coba
        Kabah
Sayil   Labna   Tulum   Island of Cozumel

GULF OF MEXICO

NORTHERN
LOWLANDS

Edzna

CAMPECHE

QUINTANA ROO

CARIBBEAN SEA

Xicalango

Candelaria River

Becan
        Rio Bec
Calakmul

Usumacinta River

Hondo River

Nohmul   Cerros
Cuello

New River

TABASCO

El Mirador   Rio Azul   Lamanai
        Nakbe   San José   Belize River
Palenque   Uaxactun   Holmul
        Piedras Negras   Tikal   Barton Ramie
        Yaxchilan   SOUTHERN
CHIAPAS   LOWLANDS
        Bonampak
                Pasión River
Altar de Sacrificios   Seibal
                Dos Pilas

NORTHERN HIGHLANDS

Lake
Izabal
                Quirigua   Naco

Izapa

Copan

SOUTHERN HIGHLANDS

PACIFIC OCEAN

Kaminaljuyu

MAYA SITES

13

the gigantic sites so familiar from tourist brochures; and here it was that they inscribed the carvings that tell their history. The Maya lowlands cover a large area: 96,500 square miles (250,000 square kilometers)—the approximate size of Pennsylvania, New York, New Jersey, and Massachusetts combined. South of the lowlands, the land rises steeply into the mountainous highlands of Guatemala and southern Mexico. This mountain zone is a tortured land, raked by several east-west mountain chains and their accompanying precipitous river valleys. Volcanic peaks, many still active, tower above the highlands, and earth-quakes periodically devastate the land. To the south of the mountain chains, the land drops steeply toward the Pacific coast. The Maya still inhabit the highland country, as they did prehistorically, but because its archaeological sites are less known—and, indeed, less spectacular—the focus of this book will be the Maya lowlands.

Mayanists traditionally divide the lowland area into northern and southern lowlands. While historically there has always been some degree of cultural dif-ference between the areas, no sharp boundary exists between the two; the dividing line is arbitrary. The northern section of the peninsula is flat, so that the Castillo at Chichen Itza looks onto a vast tableland. This almost undiffer-entiated relief is broken near the peninsula's eastern edge by the low, rolling Puuc Hills—the location of an important group of ancient sites. Moving south into Guatemala, the land is marked by limestone ridges, flanked by depres-sions, that run on a northwest-southeast diagonal. Although the ridges are not high—a few hundred feet at most—they are fairly steep, with marked ecologi-cal differences between the ridgetops, the slopes, and the depressions. The large Maya sites are invariably located in the thin but well-drained soil atop the tallest ridges; the depressions—or *bajos*—are seasonal swamps with heavy, deep soil apt to have standing water during the rainy season.

The annual pendulum of rainy and dry seasons is, indeed, the dominant feature of the lowland climate. As the thermal equator sways from north to south with the path of the sun, it is followed by trade winds and their atten-dant moisture. Rainy season in Maya country begins in May; by December, the rains become less frequent, while the period from January till the end of April is relatively dry. The amount of rainfall varies from north to south. Some locales at the dry northern tip of the Yucatan Peninsula receive as little as 20 inches (51 centimeters) of rain annually; yet farther south, the total climbs to 50 inches (127 cm) at the Guatemalan/Mexican border, then soars to a soggy 100 inches (254 cm)—or more—in the mountain chains of Guatemala. Temperatures at this latitude and elevation are necessarily tropical, varying far less than in more temperate zones. Daytime temperatures average in the 90s (32° Celsius) through the rainy season; the air cools to a refreshing mid-80s (29 to 30° C) during January and February, then rises sharply—sometimes exceed-ing 100 degrees (38° C)—in March and April. Nighttime temperatures drop only slightly, and although winter may bring chilly nights, frost is unknown.

Obtaining water during the dry season was one of the main challenges for the lowland Maya, as most of it filtered through the porous limestone and made its way into underground drainage systems. At some sites, as at Tikal, the ancient Maya built holding reservoirs. At others, they constructed chultuns—small pits, lined with plaster. In places the limestone surface actually dissolved and caved in, allowing access to the water through deep holes, called cenotes, such as this one at Dzitnup, Yucatan.

Humidity is invariably high, because of the region's ample rainfall and the moisture released—even during the dry season—from forest vegetation.

The porous limestone bedrock acts like a sponge. Rather than flowing off into streams and rivers, rainwater gurgles down through sinkholes to underground drainage systems far below the surface. As a result, obtaining water for household use during the dry season can be a severe problem for most of the interior lowlands. The ancient Maya overcame this hurdle in several ways, depending upon local circumstances. In southern lowland sites, for example, where a layer of impermeable clay prevented water from penetrating the limestone, they built large reservoirs; the site of Tikal boasts 10 such reservoirs, with a total capacity of 40 million gallons (169 million liters). In the Puuc Hills to the north, the Maya constructed hundreds of cisterns—called *chultuns*—by digging small pits into the bedrock and lining them with plaster. Across the Northern Plains, where underground drainage systems are much closer to the surface, geological evolution had provided *cenotes*: spots where the limestone surface had dissolved and caved in, providing access to water below.

Toward the fringes of the southern lowlands, the geology differs enough to permit river systems. Several rivers drain the Belize section of the lowlands to the east, while water from the southern and western edges flows into the large Pasion/Usumacinta river system. Riverbanks throughout these systems are lined with Maya sites, and in prehistoric times the water must have teemed with the canoes of traders and fisherfolk.

Tropical forest is the natural vegetation throughout much of the lowlands. Although usually called "rain forest," much of it is technically "monsoon forest"—characterized by a longer dry season than true rain forest. Gigantic trees predominate, most retaining their leaves year-round. The upper level of the multi-storied canopy towers 100 to 130 feet (30 to 40 meters) above the forest floor. This prodigious height results primarily from competition for sunlight, as opportunistic trees reach to steal sun from their neighbors. Slow-growing hardwoods are most common. Some trees—mahogany and Spanish cedar, for example—are familiar to us from furniture; but most, such as the *ramón* (breadnut) and the sapodilla (whose sap, called chicle, provided the original base for chewing gum before being replaced by plastic), are unfamiliar to temperate zone dwellers. Hundred-foot (30-meter) lianas droop to the ground, and bromeliads and orchids blossom unnoticed in the canopy, yet since the canopy is closed and sunlight rarely touches the ground, little vegetation clutters the forest floor; the only impediments to walking are the giant trees' great buttressed roots. But whenever a patch of forest is cleared, either by natural treefall or by human effort, the unaccustomed sunlight brings to life seeds that have lain dormant—often for years—causing an explosion of nearly impenetrable floor-level vegetation. As one travels northward in the Yucatan Peninsula, the trees become gradually shorter, finally giving way to a dense and thorny scrub forest.

To the visitor, the monsoon forest appears an incredibly lush and fertile environment; in fact, quite the opposite is true. The forest is actually an evolutionary answer to difficult conditions. Soil in the Maya lowlands is thin (a foot or two on top of bedrock) and poor in nutrients. Fallen leaves and branches decay rapidly, and rainwater quickly dissolves nutrients from the resultant compost, carrying them downward to the deep underground drainage systems where roots never reach. The forest's survival depends on a natural recycling system that counters this loss. Root systems spread profusely through the shallow soil, (making archaeological digging a constant struggle against a remarkable tangle of roots). As nutrients are released from decayed vegetation and carried into the soil by rainwater, they are quickly recaptured by the convoluted network of roots and carried upward to be put into storage as new vegetation.

Other adaptations protect against plant-eating insects. Unlike in temperate zones, where insect populations are destroyed by winter cold and must rebuild again each spring, temperature poses no threat to tropical insects; populations can expand to the limits set by predators and food availability. But because most herbaceous insects have fairly narrow food choices (mahogany bugs favor mahogany, for example), they proliferate only where their favorite plants abound. By scattering their various food sources, the rain forest combats rampant insect growth. Whereas temperate forest is characterized by vast stands of a single species, tropical forest mixes species, so that if one stands under a mahogany tree, the closest mahogany is likely to be far out of sight, with a dozen other varieties in between. This scattering probably happens because a concentration of predators near a mature tree prevents the survival of new seedlings. Also, most tropical plants are equipped with chemical defenses that

Much of the lowlands is covered in tropical vegetation, some of it so dense that Maya sites lay undiscovered for centuries. Tropical flowers such as these brightly colored heliconia—often used as food by the ancient Maya—compete for space in the lush monsoon forest.

16

Even enormous structures can prove very difficult to locate amid the vegetation. Here, at Guatemala's Piedras Negras, a wall is next-to-invisible behind the forest growth. What seems to be an ominous face may be an illusion or more recent phenomenon, because it is unlike Maya-style carving.

make them unpalatable—even deadly—to insects and other predators. The forest's many hallucinogens and potentially medicinal chemicals evolved as defense mechanisms—Valium, for example, was derived from a forest plant.

Compared with large open habitats such as the Great Plains of North America or the African savanna, tropical forest is not rich in mammals, especially large ones. Still, while most are hard to spot, there are populations of tapirs, jaguars, deer, and peccaries, as well as smaller animals such as howler and spider monkeys and a variety of rodents. Two of the larger tropical mammals decline rapidly when humans are present: the lumbering tapir—who leads a nocturnal lifestyle and is therefore rarely seen—and the impressive jaguar, once much desired by the Maya for its pelt. Deer and peccary fare better near humans—it has even been suggested that the Maya might have maintained herds of semi-tame peccaries—but even they must have dwindled in times of peak population.

On the other hand, tropical forest is a marvelous environment for birds. Bird-watchers swing between alternate fits of rapture and despair at the variety and elusiveness of parrots, toucans, ocellated turkeys, and thousands of smaller species coloring sky and trees. Many birds are edible and others are useful for their brightly colored feathers; yet, again, most are forest-dependent and decline as humans clear the landscape.

The tropical forest housed many animals important to both the Maya view of the universe and to their economic system. The scarlet macaw was just one of the birds whose feathers were used as adornments. The Yucatan Peninsula exported plumage of parrots, hummingbirds, and toucans to the highlands; the highlands specialized in the feathers of the quetzal, worn only by the ruling class.

But for sheer staggering variety, no category of living creature comes close to tropical insects. The species of ants alone, to say nothing of the astronomical numbers of individual members, are incalculable. Some are huge; others, mere dots. Some march in strict lines, each bearing a tiny green leafy flag; others carpet the forest floor in a devouring mass. Flying insects fill the air, day and night, causing unpleasant reactions with their bites. On the ground there are stinging scorpions, strange caterpillars, centipedes, beetles of all colors, and cockroaches as big as silver dollars. Innumerable, largely unnamed and undescribed, these smallest of the forest's inhabitants represent an enormous percentage of the world's species. The majority will become extinct before we ever knew they existed.

In this remarkable land where the early Maya worked out their destiny, many important resources—building stone, for example—existed in quantity. Covered by a hard crust, the limestone bedrock itself is soft and easily cut below the top few inches, even with the limited tools—themselves fashioned from stone—available to the Maya. The material of choice for cutting and chopping tools was chert, a flint-like rock that breaks to give sharp edges. A natural inclusion in limestone, it was easily available throughout the Yucatan Peninsula. The forest supplied a wealth of commodities: hardwoods for houses and furniture, boxes and trinkets, fuel; resin—from the copal tree—for ceremonial incense; dazzling plumes for the costumes of the elite; jaguar pelts for clothing and, fittingly, for the king's pillow covers.

Jaguars held powerful sway with the ancient Maya, and were considered companions in the sacred universe. The Maya believed that the animals served as intermediaries between the living and the dead and protected the ruling houses.

But the limestone plateau and its forest also lacked many items, a situation begetting a lively import trade. Since there was no hard stone to speak of, the Maya often imported volcanic rock from the distant highlands to make the *manos* and *metates* they used to grind corn. Another highlands import was obsidian, a black volcanic glass used to make knives sharper than surgical scalpels. Fish were unavailable except near the coast, and edible birds and animals grew scarce as the population grew. The resulting diet—almost exclusively vegetarian—provided insufficient salt to compensate for that lost through perspiration in the lowland heat, so salt, too, was imported. The Maya also imported many items used in ceremony and in jewelry-making: pigments for painting pottery and murals, seashells and coral, and jade—a Maya treasure.

While a significant thrill of Maya archaeology has always been the excitement of exploring a forested area without the aid of roads or maps, the days of such excitement are numbered. As recently as my own early days with the Tikal Project in the 1960s, nothing but forest covered the 18-mile (30-kilometer) stretch northward from Lake Peten Itza (where the only sizable modern population lived) to Tikal. Today, this forest is gone; farmsteads line a road that did not exist 30 years ago. And the colonists continue to arrive, mostly peasant farmers from land-poor sections of Guatemala. At present there remain vast areas of unoccupied forest north of Tikal. Hundreds of small sites have never been seen by archaeologists, and it is entirely possible that major sites still lie unreported. But within a generation or two, the forest will likely be gone; and, due to the predations of the looter—trafficking to the insatiable world art market—any new sites may well be devastated the instant they are discovered.

As for contemporary Maya culture, one can still hope. The collapse of Maya Classic civilization in the ninth century left much of the southern lowlands all but deserted until the last few years. Yet Maya civilization did not disappear. Even in the south, pockets of survivors carried on the old traditions, and in the northern lowlands of Yucatan and the highlands toward the Pacific, Maya culture continued into a vigorous Postclassic period that lasted until the arrival of the Spanish *conquistadores* in the 1520s. The descendants of these ancient Maya continue to live in the northern sections of the Yucatan Peninsula and in the mountainous areas of Guatemala, Belize, and the Mexican state of Chiapas. Although the structure of ancient Maya society was destroyed by the Spaniards, the Maya of today—village people, supporting themselves mainly by age-old farming systems—continue to speak Maya languages and dress daily in traditional costumes. At ceremonies, the flute and drum sound, incense from the copal tree fills the air, and the names of the ancient gods are chanted (although nowadays intermingled with those of Christian saints). Like ethnic minorities elsewhere around the world, the Maya are under pressure from the dominant culture in their area; still on the margin of the economic and political systems of Mexico and Guatemala, they must struggle to maintain their lands and customs. But the Maya have faced difficult times before, and they have survived.

Though the Maya lowlands were rich in many resources, the lack of hard stone necessitated the development of an import system. Volcanic rock was brought from the highlands to be turned into manos and metates—the implements used for processing corn, shown here in a detail from Diego Rivera's mural at Mexico City's Palacio Nacional.

The arch at Labna is one of Frederick Catherwood's engravings from the 1843 bestseller by John Lloyd Stephens, *Incidents of Travel in Yucatan*. the world of the Maya from relative obscurity to almost instant popularity.

The works of Stephens and Catherwood took

2

THE EARLY DAYS OF DISCOVERY

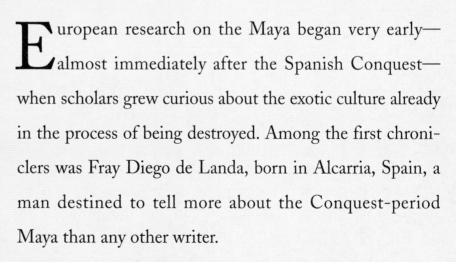

European research on the Maya began very early—almost immediately after the Spanish Conquest—when scholars grew curious about the exotic culture already in the process of being destroyed. Among the first chroniclers was Fray Diego de Landa, born in Alcarria, Spain, a man destined to tell more about the Conquest-period Maya than any other writer.

A Franciscan by the age of 17, he was still in his 20s in 1549 when he arrived with a fresh shipment of friars in

Fray Diego de Landa arrived in Mérida in 1549 to serve in a Franciscan monastery. Fanatical and ambitious, Landa later became Bishop of Yucatan, a position from which he set out to cleanse the practices of both Spaniards and Maya. In attempting to eradicate Maya "paganism," he burned countless "idols" and a number of ancient hieroglyphic books.

Mérida, Yucatan. Paintings of Landa show a proud, determined face with a strong chin and deep-set eyes; it is not a face that bespeaks gentleness. Almost from the beginning, Landa stood in the eye of his own hurricane. His ability, and his forcefulness, propelled him rapidly through a series of ecclesiastical posts until, in 1561, he was elected Yucatan Provincial: territorial head of the Franciscan order. Ambitious and talented—but also inflexible, combative, and impetuous—Landa was given to excess. Historian Angel Garibay put it this way: "The virtue most lacking in him was prudence, without which all other virtues fail."

Yucatan in the mid-16th century was a frontier where power, clerical no less than secular, was for the taking. The *encomenderos*—Spanish landholders enriched by land grants and Indian workers—set their own laws and treated their Indian subjects as they saw fit. Meanwhile the various priestly orders bickered and jockeyed for position in the new land. The Spanish crown tried to resolve disputes at both levels, but because the situation often had changed completely before proclamations reached the provinces, these royal interventions had little effect. When Landa was named Provincial, he pitched in, like an ecclesiastical Wyatt Earp, to clean house.

Beginning with the encomenderos, he lashed out from the pulpit, deriding them by name and indicting their arrangements with Indian women; some he brought to trial under charges of blasphemy, bigamy, or irreverence. Nor were the Indians exempt. Covert pagan rites—sometimes practiced by the very individuals responsible for church ceremonies—sparked the fury of the new Provincial. Landa charged that the land was riddled with idolatry—perhaps a not-unfounded allegation. With his customary vigor, he initiated thorough investigations, during which flagging memories were refreshed by torture. Confessions poured forth. Yes, idols had been worshipped; human beings had been sacrificed—even in churches. Idols by the hundreds were turned over to the friars, although a later document suggests that many of them had been manufactured expressly to satisfy the clergy's insatiable appetite. The culmination of Landa's campaign was a judicial proceeding of the Inquisition, an *auto-da-fé* held in the village of Mani. Scores of idols were torched in a gigantic pyre, and offenders were sentenced en masse, most to fines, public penance, or long periods of labor. Yet what most besmirched Landa's name was not his cruel treatment of human offenders, but the burning of books of hieroglyphic writing, known as codices. His description of the event torments scholars to this day:

> We found a large number of books of these characters and, as they contained nothing in which there were not to be seen superstition and lies of the devil, we burned them all which they regretted to an amazing degree and which caused them much affliction.

Landa's zeal was too great even for those times: He was accused of mismanagement, and of exceeding his authority. Enraged, he resigned his posts and left for Spain to defend himself before the authorities. It was there, probably in

1566, that Landa wrote his *Relación de las Cosas de Yucatán* (Account of the Things of Yucatan). By far the most important chronicle of the Spanish expeditions—or *entradas*—in the Maya area, this document is a paradox. Although devised to justify the extreme measures Landa had taken—including torture—the *Relación* is a moderate, scholarly work whose pages shine with enthusiasm and respect for the land, its plants and animals, and the customs of its people.

The book reflects the mixture of horror, awe, and admiration with which the Spaniards viewed Maya culture. They were particularly dismayed by Maya religious practices. Even though religious violence was rife in Europe, the executions and burnings back home had not prepared the Conquistadors for blood-splattered Maya priests tearing hearts from still-living sacrificial victims. Still, the Spaniards marveled at the pomp and splendor of Maya leaders, and were awed by the size of local settlements; they recognized traces of an earlier splendor in the ruins of already-ancient sites. Landa observed:

> For it is true that in its buildings and the multitude of them it is the most remarkable of all the things which up to this day have been discovered in the Indies; for they are so many in number and so many are the parts of the country where they are found, and so well built are they of cut stone in their fashion, that it fills one with astonishment....

> And as this country, although it is a good land, is not at present such as it appears to have been in the prosperous time, when so many and such remarkable buildings were built, without their having any kind of metal with which to build them...that except to those who have seen them, it will seem to be jesting to tell about them.

But the ruins visible to the Spanish were but a tiny fraction of those that had existed, for all of the sites in the southern part of the lowlands were still lost in the miles of trackless forest that would not be explored for many years to come.

Landa, of course, was not alone in his fascination with the Maya. A number of other scholars of the 16th and 17th centuries have left accounts of Maya customs and history, some borrowing liberally from Landa's manuscript before it fell into oblivion. (A copy was rediscovered in the Academia de Historia in Madrid in 1863 by the Abbé Brasseur de Bourbourg, a priest who had been stationed in Maya communities in Guatemala and had become an avid student of Maya culture and history). It was almost certainly during the 16th century that the three—or possibly four—surviving prehispanic Maya codices were shipped to Europe (the authenticity of the fourth codex is still debated); but these appear to have been deemed mere curiosities, as no account of them survives from the time. Like Landa's *Relación*, they also had to await rediscovery several centuries later.

The 17th and 18th centuries saw no substantial studies of the Maya, although what might be called archaeology began in the late 18th century. On

While on a visit to London, John Lloyd Stephens (*above*), a New York lawyer and travel writer, met architect Frederick Catherwood whose panoramas Stephens admired. The two spent years together exploring Central America and from their writing and sketching on these Maya journeys came two of the mid-1800s' bestselling books.

hearing of the Palenque site, the devoted antiquarian Charles III of Spain dispatched two men—both actually artillery captains—to excavate: first, Antonio del Río, then later, Guillermo Dupaix. But their reports received little immediate scholarly attention, and were not published until the second quarter of the 19th century.

JOHN LLOYD STEPHENS AND HIS ECCENTRIC CONTEMPORARIES

Into the 1830s, then, the Maya remained obscure, known only to a small group of scholars and the most adventuresome of travelers. But the Maya soon were to be rescued from obscurity by the splendid prose of John Lloyd Stephens, a New York lawyer turned travel writer. Born in New Jersey in 1805, Stephens graduated from Columbia College at 17, then briefly practiced law on Wall Street until a friend at Harper & Brothers publishers suggested a quick route to fame and fortune: travel accounts. Stephens' first book, on Europe and the Middle East, brought him instant success and financial independence; now in search of new challenges, he set his sights on visiting the still-untamed wilds of Central America, along with its fabled ruins. Meanwhile, in London, an unsuccessful architect named Frederick Catherwood had turned to producing vast painted panoramas to which the British flocked in the mid-19th century. Stephens, on a visit to London, was impressed by Catherwood's panorama of Jerusalem; he introduced himself and the men became friends. As Stephens' plans to visit the Maya ruins matured, he invited Catherwood to join him as artist.

As part of his plan, Stephens accepted a diplomatic appointment as U.S. emissary to a new Central American confederation—a confederation that dissolved into chaos before he even reached his destination. Arriving in Belize in 1839, Stephens and Catherwood spent the next 10 months exploring the wilderness. Travel was an adventure in itself. Central America was perpetually war-torn, beset by roving bands of government supporters and insurgents who fought a seesaw battle to control countries and confederacies whose boundaries changed from day to day. Stephens tells of mule trips along muddy trails with unreliable supplies, of guides and muleteers apt to disappear at any stop. Despite the hazards, Stephens and Catherwood reached Copan in Western Honduras, then trekked overland to Uxmal. Fighting the jungle and insects (the account tells of Catherwood sketching in foot-deep mud, wearing gloves against the mosquitoes), they produced notes and drawings that charmed the public; their collaborative volume became an instant bestseller in 1841, and was soon translated into six languages. An 1843 volume, about a second Maya journey, enjoyed equal success.

Antiquarianism, and a nascent archaeology, had taken the public's fancy in the early 19th century. Egypt had led the way. When Napoleon embarked upon his campaign to conquer Egypt in 1798, he took with him 175 "learned civilians"—the scientific elite of the day. This contingent diligently (and ruthlessly) collected antiquities, and Napoleon himself was so impressed by the aura of

Copan, Honduras, was the first Maya site visited by Stephens and Catherwood. To avoid troubles with the landlord, they purchased the site for $50 U.S. Shown here is the modern view of the now-reconstructed ball court.

ancient Egypt that in one exhortation to his troops he pointed to the pyramids, saying, "Soldiers, forty centuries are looking down upon you." Within a few years, the young French linguistic prodigy Jean-François Champollion had deciphered the Egyptian hieroglyphs with the aid of the Rosetta Stone, whose trilingual inscriptions were in Egyptian hieroglyphs; a second, simplified, Egyptian script; and Greek. Soon after, the glories of Mesopotamia joined the vogue. Stephens' achievement was to give America a civilization of its own, complete with a romantic setting—for the ruins deep in a dense tropical forest seemed somehow more mysterious than those in the windswept desert. He writes:

> Who were the people that built this city?...The place where we were sitting, was it a citadel from which an unknown people had sounded the trumpet of war? or a temple for the worship of the God of peace?... All was mystery, dark, impenetrable mystery... In Egypt the colossal skeletons of gigantic temples stand in unwatered sands in all the nakedness of desolation; but here an immense forest shrouds the ruins, hiding them from sight, heightening the impression and moral effect, and giving an intensity and almost wildness to the interest.... Here were the remains of a cultivated, polished and peculiar people, who had passed through all the stages incidental to the rise and fall of nations, reached their golden age and perished, entirely unknown.

Whether or not the public was tiring of camels and sand and Bedouins, the Maya were a sensation; they became a lively topic of conversation among educated Europeans and Americans.

Uxmal, with its impressive Nunnery Quadrangle, is located in the Puuc region of the Yucatan. Comparatively few inscriptions adorn Puuc buildings. From the lack of inscriptions and different architectural style, Stephens and Catherwood deduced that the Puuc culture represented a different or later culture than that of such Classic sites as Copan and Palenque.

The Maya could not have fared better. Stephens was a careful and sober observer in an epoque of fanciful speculation; and yet the mud, the ruins, the mystery, all come alive. The aura of the Maya envelops the reader. And Stephens never doubted that the ancient ruins had been constructed by the ancestors of the modern inhabitants of the area—not by Phoenicians or the Lost Tribes of Israel. Looking at the hieroglyphic inscriptions and carvings of the stone slabs, called stelae, Stephens recognized that they told the history of the Maya. Musing upon a stela at Copan, he notes:

> We considered that in the medallion tablets the people who reared it had published a record of themselves, through which we might one day hold a conference with a perished race, and unveil the mystery that hung over the city.

Catherwood's drawings similarly exuded a romantic charm, but were executed with a faithfulness that did not distort the originals. This solid, if romantic, realism of Stephens and Catherwood was a welcome contrast to the reports that had preceded their books. Previously, the jungles of Maya country were being presented to the world by a succession of dubious adventurer/explorers who, after thrashing through the forest like a troop of

In keeping with the newly stirred interest in Central American explorations, the Chicago World's Fair of 1933-34 contained this full-scale replica of the Nunnery at Uxmal. An expedition to Uxmal was made specifically to gather the data and make the drawings from which the replica was constructed.

demented Boy Scouts, sought fame and fortune by spinning fabulous tales. Some were charlatans; some, madmen; others, both. At their best, these archaeological apostles did, indeed, provide new information about Maya ruins, but ultimately fact became so confused with delusion that the two could no longer be separated. Still, these eccentric individuals were not devoid of charm and color.

Before Stephens had arrived in Maya country, it had already been visited by one such memorable figure. He called himself Count Jean-Frédéric Waldeck. He had been born, he claimed, in 1766, variously in Paris, Prague, or Vienna (the location depended upon when and by whom he was asked). In his illustrious youth, Waldeck had participated in famous expeditions to Africa and the Indian Ocean; he had accompanied Napoleon to Egypt—yet, strangely enough, a diligent search of the records of any of these expeditions fails to reveal his name. What *can* be verified is that he lived and worked at Palenque in 1832 and 1833, then moved to Uxmal, where he labored for many years. Everywhere the count looked in the ruins, he saw the handiwork of Egyptians or Hindus or Chaldeans; he was obsessed with elephants, which he recognized time and again in the Maya carvings. He discovered, to his own great satisfaction, that the courtyard of the Nunnery at Uxmal was paved with 56,946 stones, each carved with the likeness of a turtle. Back in Europe at age 84, he married his housekeeper's niece and promptly fathered a child. Later, having passed the age of 100, he boastfully proclaimed: "I have passed the age when

Very little of the colorful life of Count Jean-Frédéric Waldeck can be verified. A larger-than-life character who worked in the 1830s at Palenque and Uxmal, he attributed those sites to Hindus, Egyptians, or Chaldeans.

Augustus Le Plongeon was an eccentric 19th-century adventurer, one of several explorers of the period to hold the theory that there were close links between the Maya and the ancient Egyptians; they both had pyramids, temples, hieroglyphic writing, and deep reverence for the sun. Although he produced new data, most of his theories were rejected by scientists.

man dies. Now there is no reason that my life should end. My archaeological studies make me believe that I have reached a state of petrifaction which can endure centuries after centuries."

But this prophecy would prove no more realistic than Waldeck's other fancies; immortality was cut short at age 109, when he is said to have turned too rapidly to follow the passage of a pretty demoiselle in Paris—and was struck down by a carriage. (A more sober version of his demise was given by his wife, but the apocryphal version better fits his character.)

Augustus Le Plongeon was cut from the same mold as Waldeck, although he seems to have been less of a charlatan. He was simply more deluded. Irascible and paranoid, Le Plongeon was a commanding, patriarchal figure with an endless beard that had turned snow-white by the time he reached the Maya area. Born on the Isle of Jersey in 1826 and well educated in Paris, Le Plongeon turned up in Marysville, California, as city surveyor in 1849. Subsequently he worked as a photographer—a field in which he showed considerable skill—then turned his hand for a time to the practice of law, and then medicine, although it is unclear whether he had formal training in either of those two professions. After an eight-year sojourn in South America—where he started a hospital and wrote unsuccessful books on photography, the Jesuits in Peru, and the Inca—he went to Yucatan in 1873; there he spent seven years working at a variety of sites, including Uxmal and Chichen Itza.

To his credit, Le Plongeon produced new data and amassed collections of artifacts. On the other hand, his ideas grew more and more fantastic, while he grew ever angrier as his speculations were rejected by scientists. Le Plongeon was convinced that the Maya was the most ancient of civilizations, estimating that Chichen Itza and Uxmal were 12,000 years old. The Maya, he alleged, had sent colonies across the Pacific to found the civilizations of Egypt and Mesopotamia. By comparing Maya inscriptions with the letters from ancient languages of the Near East, he achieved a milestone by being the first to claim success in reading them, and informed the world that Egyptian hieroglyphs were one-third Maya. Le Plongeon was aided in this effort—so he said—when he discovered a roomful of ancient Maya manuscripts (the location of which he refused to disclose). His indignation was more than evident in 1881 when he addressed the American Antiquarian Society and proclaimed spitefully:

> ...since I felt that I was abandoned by all, notwithstanding all wanted to procure from me gratis what had cost me so much time, labor and money to acquire, I made up my mind to keep my knowledge, so dearly purchased, to destroy some day or other my collections and to let those who wish to know more about the ancient cities of Yucatan, do what I have done...

His decipherments led to a story of a Maya Queen named Móo, her husband, Chacmool—the ruler of Chichen Itza—and Chacmool's brother and

Teobert Maler, after a stint with the Mexican imperial army in the mid-1800s, stayed on in the area, taking remarkable photographs of Maya villages and ruins such as this view of the east face of the palace at Palenque. He always developed his work in the field and would patiently rephotograph until he met his own exacting standards.

high priest, Cay. The exploits of these imaginary Maya, bursting with intrigue and murder, colored the pages of a book entitled *Queen Móo and the Egyptian Sphinx*. Augustus Le Plongeon died in 1908 at the age of 83, still clinging to his interpretations and decrying the conspiracies of his fellow archaeologists.

THE RISE OF SERIOUS STUDIES

Out of the naïveté and wild fabrications of the 19th century, a new, legitimate profession was to spring. Archaeology began to attract scholars who were more interested in genuine research than in scratching together evidence to substantiate romantic delusions. In Egypt and the Near East, this development fostered increasing rigor in large-scale excavations, leading to the decipherment, one after another, of ancient scripts. In Maya country, the new generation of explorer-archaeologists who followed Stephens and his bizarre contemporaries were more sober, each more professional than the last. Their tools were cameras and mapping equipment; their objective, to discover and report. These new adventurers generated scientific monographs rather than popular books. Archaeology was coming of age.

Two men typified this new breed. Teobert Maler, born in Rome of German parents, enlisted as a very young man in the ill-fated army of Maximilian in his brief sojourn as emperor of Mexico. Maler chose to stay and travel in Mexico, and, entranced by a visit to Palenque where he met already-established explorers, decided to devote himself to a study of the ruins. Settling in Yucatan in 1888

29

This dramatic photograph of the tower at Palenque was taken by Alfred Maudslay in 1889.

at the age of 46, he was to spend the next 20 years in a series of expeditions, first throughout Yucatan, then farther south along the Usumacinta River and into the Peten, the northernmost department—equivalent to a U.S. state—in Guatemala. The Peabody Museum of Harvard University sponsored some of Maler's explorations, publishing the results in its "Memoirs" series. But as time went on, Maler became more and more recalcitrant in matters of publication, perhaps because he suspected the museum of selling his reports at a great profit. Peabody ceased its support and Maler, who stayed on in Yucatan, became more and more embittered and eccentric until his death in 1917.

Alfred Percival Maudslay, a Cambridge-educated Englishman of independent means, paralleled Maler's crotchety path, although in a more affable manner. A restless traveler in his youth, Maudslay visited Quirigua in 1881 and became infected with the dangerous madness that lurks in the jungle, leaving its victims with an insatiable hunger to study the Maya. He abandoned all other plans, and devoted eight seasons over the next 13 years to the exploration and recording of Maya sites. Clearer than Maler about his objectives, Maudslay hoped to provide a record that could contribute to further study of the Maya. He would achieve his goal: He drew and photographed with such skill that, even today, one can still return with profit to his photographs for details of buildings and decoration that have since eroded away. Maudslay also devoted enormous effort to making plaster casts of stelae, again

Alfred Percival Maudslay, a Cambridge-educated Englishman who gave up a diplomatic career to pursue his interest in archaeology, is seen here at work inside one of the vaulted rooms at Chichen Itza. He was a meticulous investigator and a skilled photographer and illustrator whose records of buildings, sculpture, and inscriptions were incorporated into the five-volume *Biologia Centrali-Americana,* which is still a useful reference work today.

to provide a permanent record. Maudslay was assisted by Annie Hunter, the first woman to have an impact in Maya studies. She produced wonderfully accurate drawings of the inscriptions.

The work of Maler, Maudslay, and several others who visited and described Maya ruins provided a much sharper concept of what the ancient sites had been like. Accurate photographs and drawings—both of major structures and of an ever-growing corpus of carved inscriptions from the Classic period—were becoming available for study. Scholars at last had something to work with.

One of the great accomplishments of 19th-century scholarship was the decipherment—authentic this time—of ancient scripts. Champollion's obsession, and the 1799 discovery of the Rosetta Stone, had led to the decoding of hieroglyphs in the 1820s. By mid-century, the great trilingual inscription that the Persian king Darius had left on the cliffs of Behistun, in present-day Iran, provided material to crack the Assyrian script. Scholars waited breathlessly as the histories of Egypt and the Near East began to emerge from contemporary accounts written in ancient times. It was natural that Maya hieroglyphic writing also began to attract the attention of scholars by the late 19th century. Yet the Maya texts presented a vexing problem because there were no multilingual inscriptions. Although Maya hieroglyphic writing was still used at the time of the Spanish Conquest, its association with the native religion resulted in the persecution of its users. Knowledge of the system was soon lost, and Maya writing became a dead script with no clues to aid in its decipherment. Mercifully, a series of 19th-century discoveries provided new materials for scholars interested in the glyphs. The three long-forgotten Maya codices were rediscovered, exhumed from their dusty European hiding places, and published in copies adequate for study. In addition, the publications of early explorers enlarged the body of Classic-period inscriptions. And, finally, Landa's *Relación de las Cosas de Yucatán*, which had not been seen since the 16th century, was rediscovered in Madrid and published in 1864.

The *Relación* was particularly exciting because it included an "alphabet" that matched Maya glyphs with sounds. Here, it seemed, was the hoped-for Rosetta Stone: One might simply plug in the sounds and read the manuscripts. Charles Étienne Brasseur de Bourbourg, the outstanding scholar and avid bibliophile who had found the Landa manuscript and a series of other important documents, addressed himself to the task. "In his enthusiasm," notes David Kelley in his history of Maya decipherment, "he attempted an entire translation of one of the codices which he subsequently admitted was unlikely to be correct, as he was reading backwards." But even when scholars read the text in the right direction, they had no greater luck; and other applications of the Landa alphabet were equally hapless. They elicited only gibberish that bore no relationship to any known language.

In the meantime, however, there was considerable progress in unraveling the Maya calendrical system. Landa's manuscript did prove useful in this task, because it supplied an accurate list and drawings of the glyphs for calendrical periods, as well as notes about mathematical notation and the different kinds of Maya calendars. Armed with this information, researchers dug into number-crunching. The codices were a gold mine for mathematical juggling; long tables of dates and numbers were accompanied by intricate instructions from the ancient scribes about counting forward and backward to reach particular dates. As work proceeded, dates piled upon dates—days numbering in the millions were faithfully counted forward or backward according to Maya instruction, and the structure of the Maya calendars emerged. Once the calendrical counts could be recognized and read, they provided a chronological yardstick for the dates in Classic-period inscriptions. The correlation of the Maya and European calendars remained a problem, because although some Colonial events dated in our calendar were also recorded in the Maya calendar, several alternative correlations were possible; none emerged as the consensus choice. Meanwhile, notwithstanding the progress in deciphering the calendar, non-calendrical glyphs remained intractable, and were not deciphered for another half century.

The first five decades of the 20th century were marked by a steady enrichment of basic knowledge about ancient Maya civilization. The exploration and description of sites continued, with special emphasis upon the recovery and recording of inscriptions, whose now-readable dates gave a clue to the development of Maya Classic civilization. Also, research into the evolution of pottery styles led to ceramic sequences—detailed descriptions of stylistic characteristics at successive stages in time—that served as a dating tool for parts of sites that lacked dated monuments. Huge quantities of data were amassed from large-scale research projects that devoted years to the investigation and reconstruction of individual sites. The layer-cake form of Maya sites became clear—level after level of construction was superimposed one atop the other—and the techniques to study the long sequences of architectural development

Very few Maya codices (manuscripts written in hieroglyphs) have survived, mainly because of their near-total destruction by the Spanish. The paper of a Maya codex was made from the inner bark of a certain type of fig tree and then covered with lime paint. The hieroglyphs were inscribed in red or black, and the accompanying pictures were drawn in black, sometimes heightened with color or placed on a colored ground. The example shown here is from the Grolier Codex, a recently appeared manuscript whose authenticity is still debated.

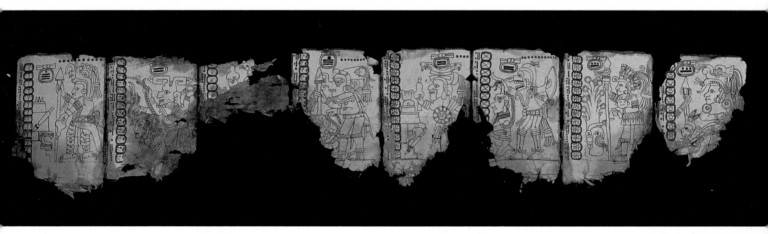

MAYA MATHEMATICS AND CALENDRICS

The ancient Maya are justly famed for their accomplishments in mathematics and calendrics. However, many of the initial inventions in these intellectual fields may not really have been of Maya origin. Calendrical dates that include mathematical notations are found earliest—in the second or third centuries B.C.—in areas probably not inhabited by the Maya along the gulf and Pacific coasts of Mesoamerica (the anthropologist's term for the area covered by the civilizations of Mexico and Central America). Nevertheless, it was the Maya who perfected the calendar; it is their inscriptions that show it in its most elaborate form. Here is a quick introduction to Maya mathematics and a summary of the highly complex calendrical system.

In mathematics, the Maya used a system of positional notation in which each position had an increasingly higher value. The concept was like that of our own positional system—which is of Arab origin—in which, for example, the number 729 indicates nine units of one, two units of tens, and seven units of hundreds. A system of positional notation must have a symbol for zero: One could not write, say, 730 without a zero to show that the ones-unit position was empty. Our positional system is decimal—using a base of ten—so that the lowest level units are ones, the next level tens, the next hundreds, and so forth. The Maya, on the other hand, employed a vigesimal system in which the base was 20; thus, while the units in the position of lowest value are ones—as in the Arabic system—those in the second place are twenties, those in third place are four hundreds (20 twenties), those in fourth place are eight thousands (20 four hundreds), etc. To indicate the quantity of units in each position—equivalent to our numerals—the Maya used dots for ones and bars for fives, while zero was indicated with a shell-shaped symbol.

The Maya calendar was nothing if not complicated. In a way roughly parallel to our own, the calendar took note of each day according to several different counts. For example, when we say, "Sunday, June 13, 1993," we are aware of where that day fell according to three different measures. First, it fell on the "Sunday position" of a seven-day count that cycles endlessly; second, on the "June 13" position of a 365-day count (366 in leap years) that also repeats endlessly; third, in the year 1993—a unique year that will not repeat, and which counts from our agreed-upon starting point originally intended to mark the birth of Christ. The Maya had two cyclical counts, vaguely similar to our day and date.

One cycle was a 260-day count, consisting of 13 numbers and 20 names. (To avoid confusing the reader with actual Maya day-names—"Ik," for example—I will simplify things by using the Roman letters A, B, C, etc., to T.) Both numbers and names advanced at the same time, so that day 1A was followed by 2B, then 3C, etc. After 13M, the number cycle was complete and started anew, while the day-names—represented here as letters—still continued; thus, the day following 13M was 1N. When the last day-name (T) was reached, it was the day 7T, but while the numerical cycle was not yet exhausted, the names began over again on 8A. After 260 days (13 numbers multiplied by 20 names), the calendar returned to the starting day 1A. This 260-day count had great ceremonial significance, and each of the 260 days corresponded to its own god.

The second cyclical count consisted of 365 days, divided into 18 months of 20 days each, with a short month of five days at the end. The months operated like our own; that is, when the month Pop began, one counted through the 20 days of Pop, then went on to the next month. The short month was undoubtedly designed to bring the count to 365, the closest whole day-count to the length of the solar year. The Maya had no leap years

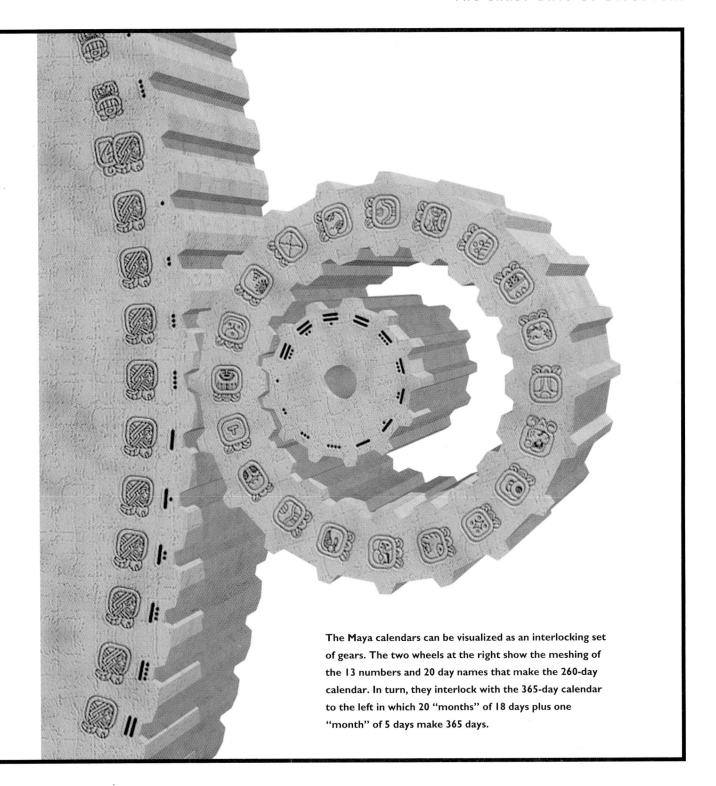

The Maya calendars can be visualized as an interlocking set of gears. The two wheels at the right show the meshing of the 13 numbers and 20 day names that make the 260-day calendar. In turn, they interlock with the 365-day calendar to the left in which 20 "months" of 18 days plus one "month" of 5 days make 365 days.

or other mechanisms to adjust the 365-day calendar to the solar year. Each year, then, a quarter of a day was lost to the sun. As a result, each individual day drifted slowly around the solar year, so that a particular day of a particular month would coincide with a particular day in the solar year—the summer solstice, say—every 1,460 (365 x 4) years; since only a quarter of a day was lost each year, the same solar day would remain at the same calendar spot for four years in a row.

The Maya named each day according to both cyclical counts, so that a date such as 1 Ik 1 Pop indicates that the 260-day count stood at 1 Ik (Ik, you may recall, is one of the 20 day-names that I earlier symbolized in letter form), while the 365-day count stood at 1 Pop. Because of the permutations of the two counts, the day 1 Ik 1 Pop would not occur again until 52 "years" of 365 days had passed. This 52-year cycle is called the Calendar Round and, as one might expect, the double New Year's day at which both cycles reached their starting points on the same day was celebrated as a very special occasion indeed.

Finally, the Maya had yet another calendar. Called the Long Count, this system enumerated days in such a way that accorded each a unique designation that would never occur again.

A calendar of this sort requires a fixed starting point—analogous to the purported birth of Christ in our calendar—and a count of elapsed time. The starting point for the Maya calendar was August 11, 3114 B.C. This mythical date, occurring far before the Maya had even begun calendrical computations, presumably represented the day on which the present universe was created. From that starting point, the Maya counted the number of days that had elapsed, recording them with their positional system of notation. The lowest position in the Long Count records 24-hour days; each day is called a *kin*, and 20 kins make a month, called a *uinal*. The Maya deviated from their vigesimal numeration system for the Long Count, counting only 18 uinals instead of 20; 18 uinals are called a *tun*. This way, instead of a total of 400 days, each tun contains 360 days, the closest multiple of 20 to the number of days in the solar year. But then the system became vigesimal again: 20 tuns equal a *katun*, an important interval because the end of a katun was a traditional point at which to dedicate a stela. Twenty katuns made a *baktun* (400 360-day years), the largest number regularly recorded in carving. A Maya date, then, might look like the one illustrated, using bar and dot numbers and the glyphs for periods

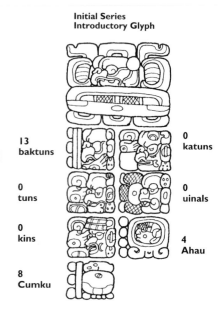

Initial Series Introductory Glyph

13 baktuns

0 katuns

0 tuns

0 uinals

0 kins

4 Ahau

8 Cumku

arranged in two columns. Many inscriptions on stelae begin with what is called an Initial Series, a long and abstruse dating formula commemorating the date on which the stela was dedicated. The formula begins with a large Introductory Glyph, saying, in effect, "Here comes a date." Then comes the Long Count—indicating the year—followed by the position that the day in question has reached in the 260 cycle. Next come references to three other cycles whose intricacies are beyond our scope: first, the name of the "Lord of the Night"—one of nine gods who shared a nine-day cycle of their own; second, an entry specifying the position of the moon;

LEFT: This Long Count calendrical inscription from Quirigua Stela C gives the starting date of the Maya calendar, a date equivalent to August 11, 3114 B.C. The Long Count runs for more than 5000 years before beginning a new cycle; the first new cycle since the 3114 date will begin on December 23, 2012 A.D.

RIGHT: This is a Long Count date from a lintel at Yaxchilan. Instead of the usual glyphs for calendrical periods and bar and dot notation for numbers, this lintel uses "full-figure" forms, alternate and more elaborate ways of writing glyphs.

third, an indication of the position in an additional cycle of 819 days (sometimes omitted, this cycle must have had numerological significance, as it fails to correspond to any astronomical phenomenon). Finally, the inscription acknowledged the position that the day occupied in the 365-day cycle. Once inscribed in its entirety, this Initial Series date served as a base for further calculations: Most other dates referred to in the same stela are indicated by instructions to count forward or backward a specified number of days from the base date. After all, who can blame the Maya for taking the odd shortcut?

were perfected. The focus of almost all projects, however, continued to be in the hearts of sites where the most impressive buildings and the majority of inscriptions were found.

SYLVANUS G. MORLEY AND THE CARNEGIE INSTITUTION

Early in this century, Sylvanus Griswold Morley took to Maya studies; he was to rule the field for a generation. Born in Chester, Pennsylvania, in 1883, Morley took his undergraduate degree in engineering, then entered graduate school at Harvard to pursue his real love: archaeology. He was sent to Chichen Itza in 1907 to draw and measure structures, and attacked the site with such abandon that for the first few days he refused to stop working long enough for a mid-day meal. His local assistant and interpreter—who also found himself subjected to a day-long fast—eventually delivered a stern lecture backed by biblical references indicating the horrid fates of those who failed to eat lunch. But Morley was irrepressible; he had been smitten by Maya archaeology and had begun the relentless dash for results that was to be his trademark.

Only five-foot-seven, sporting a small mustache and a thatch of unruly hair that tumbled over his forehead, Morley was, in the words of his friend and colleague J. Eric S. Thompson, "of indifferent physique." He was helpless without his large, round spectacles, although he most often removed them to pose for photographs. In the field, Morley wore an absurd peasant sombrero whose peak towered far above him and which frequently tumbled off as he bounced through the forest. He spoke in a high-pitched, nasal voice, with an accent that he himself attributed to Pennsylvania but that others claimed had no known equivalent in the English-speaking world. In what remained an unending mystery to his male companions, women found Morley irresistible.

Morley was a master of two sorts of archaeological enterprise. A superb diplomat, he excelled in fund-raising and in getting permission to start large projects; then, in the forest, he was capable of spending months at a stretch on lonely trips, avidly recording sites and inscriptions. His success at diplomatic maneuvering began early. In 1912, the Carnegie Institution of Washington—a prestigious foundation with a large endowment—was being pushed by a member of its board of directors to start a branch that would investigate Central American archaeology. Morley heard of Carnegie's interest, and presented a proposal for a major project at Chichen Itza, in Mexico. After a controversial competition—which made him some lasting enemies—Morley was offered a job with Carnegie at $200 per month. By that time, however, relationships between the United States and Mexico had soured, effectively postponing any large project. So Morley undertook the first of his several periodic searches for inscriptions under Carnegie auspices. It was, in fact, a dozen years before work at Chichen Itza was to start; World War 1,

Sylvanus G. Morley, seen in this circa 1910 photo in the west doorway of the Temple of the Initial Series at Chichen Itza, was a Harvard-educated archaeologist and one of the most influential and dedicated Mayanists of the 20th century. His infectious enthusiasm and energy led to the creation of major field projects at a variety of Maya sites.

revolution in Mexico, and time-consuming diplomatic arrangements all intervened. Finally, in 1924, the Chichen Project got under way. Over the next 13 years the work produced a series of major revelations that laid the foundation for our modern understanding of sites in northern Yucatan. In 1926, two years after the start of the Chichen Project, the Carnegie Institution also moved into Guatemala, embarking on a large project at the site of Uaxactun.

In both projects, Morley showed a gift for attracting people of talent who were to become the leading Maya archaeologists of the generation to follow. But although Morley's diplomacy was invaluable, Carnegie began to doubt both his administrative reliability and his research objectives; Karl Ruppert, an architect whom Morley had hired in the second season at Chichen, was appointed field head at Chichen Itza. Morley, meanwhile, was told to concentrate on research and writing. Later, in 1929, Carnegie appointed A.V. Kidder—then known best for his contributions to archaeology in the U.S. Southwest—as director of a newly created Historical Section; once again, somebody had been moved ahead of Morley in the administrative hierarchy.

Morley's own research was almost entirely devoted to the discovery and recording of carved inscriptions. Season after season, he took improbable trips through the forest, visiting new sites reported to him by chicle gatherers, who explored widely for trees containing the sap for chewing gum (he offered $25 U.S. for directions to each new inscription). Despite his hardiness, Morley

El Castillo Pyramid at Chichen Itza sits at the center of a broad open plaza. For about 300 years after the collapse of more southerly lowland cities, Chichen Itza ranked first among a group of northern lowland centers of commerce and religion before fading from glory. The Carnegie Institution project at Chichen Itza, organized by Sylvanus Morley, was the first major project at a Maya site.

loathed the forest, and is reported to have said that "only liars and damned fools say they like the jungle." Robert Brunhouse, Morley's biographer, notes:

> Vay (as Morley was called) lived in mortal fear of snakes; he searched his cot at night, imagined he heard them slithering nearby as he went off to sleep, and insisted that he felt their presence as his mule passed through the marshy ground of a *bajo*.

Two publications were to become Morley's masterpieces. In 1920, a massive two-volume tome called *The Inscriptions at Copán* came out in the Carnegie publication series. In 1937, *The Inscriptions of Petén*—a five-volume set complete with maps and meticulous drawings—reported on the sites Morley had visited in his long journeys through the forest. Morley's intention was to provide a record for the future. Indeed, he did so, and dog-eared copies of the volumes he authored are still pulled off library shelves time and again by researchers. Beyond his invaluable basic record, Morley contributed largely to the understanding of the calendrical portion of the inscriptions; in the interpretation of non-calendrical glyphs, however, his efforts were as fruitless as those of other investigators.

The Carnegie projects at Chichen Itza and Uaxactun revolutionized Maya archaeology. Both projects were larger in scale and involved substantially more excavation than anything attempted before; both were to last 13 years, a sacred

Maya number. But, as Stephen Black has noted in his history of Carnegie archaeological research, the two undertakings were very different in character and objective. Morley's favorite—the project with which he was personally involved—was at Chichen Itza. The work there aimed at providing an understanding of the later periods in Yucatan, what Morley called the "New Empire." Chichen was large, spectacular, and, since it was already a popular destination for travelers, a primary aim was reconstruction of the site as a tourist attraction. Not that the archaeology was insignificant, of course. Loving care was lavished on architectural details; new carvings and murals were uncovered, old ones put back in shape; and a massive attempt was made to link the site with the native chronicles of the Maya in Yucatan. All work was carried out gingerly, with an eye to the final product: a splashy site restored and refurbished for tourism.

Uaxactun was different. It was dug to give Carnegie insight into the "Old Empire": the Classic period whose sites filled the untrammeled forests of the Peten in northern Guatemala. Less well preserved than Chichen—and so remote that it seemed unlikely ever to attract visitors—Uaxactun was, in a sense, expendable. Besides, only 12 miles (19 kilometers) from the giant and eye-catching Tikal, it could therefore serve as a training ground for eventual work at its more spectacular neighbor. In effect, Uaxactun seemed the sort of place one might dig unhampered, worrying about nothing but research results. Stephen Black puts it this way:

> Carnegie...secured a concession from the government of Guatemala for the right to spend five years carrying out a unique experiment: to dig up Uaxactun as no other Maya site had before or has since been dug. No reconstruction, no tourists, few restrictions, and not much advance planning ("research design") about what should be done, just Morley's conviction that excavations at Uaxactun would reveal the development and grandeur of the Old Empire Maya.

The Uaxactun project, then, was pure research; its results were spectacular. But while a superbly detailed knowledge of architectural change came to light as whole complexes of buildings were peeled off layer by layer, the remains of later structures were unceremoniously dumped in backdirt. A ceramic sequence was worked out, providing a means to date each layer. Burial after burial was discovered and carefully recorded. The discovery of the wonderfully preserved early building known as E-VII sub (so-named because it was hidden beneath the structure whose map designation was E-VII) pushed the beginning of Maya ceremonial construction back much further than anyone would have guessed. But then E-VII sub was left to decay in the tropical rains. One could no longer do a project the way Uaxactun was done, because our sense of archaeological preservation is now too strongly developed. Nowadays Carnegie is criticized for its "depredations," but in the 1920s nobody really thought it important that

Uaxactun, once studied, should be preserved. In terms of their methodology, however, it must be said that the Uaxactun archaeologists were meticulous; they set standards of careful reporting and attention to stratigraphy that fundamentally changed archaeology in the Maya lowlands.

J. ERIC S. THOMPSON

In 1925, Morley offered a job at Chichen Itza to a young man who was to prove his successor as the major figure in Maya studies. J. Eric S. Thompson brought to the field the sophistication of the British upper classes. The son of a Harley Street physician, Thompson had served in the trenches of France in World War 1 before receiving a Cambridge education. Under Morley's tutelage, he cut his archaeological teeth on the friezes at Chichen's Temple of the Warriors, then moved to Belize, where he undertook a series of other archaeological projects.

Thompson's interests were broader than Morley's. Eschewing the focus on the large and spectacular that dominated Maya archaeology, he directed a project at the small site of San José to discover how the ordinary Maya had lived. At the same time, he became fascinated with the contemporary Maya, with whom he spent long days of travel through the bush and shared evening campfires; not all old beliefs and customs, concluded Thompson, were dead. His first monograph, in fact, was an ethnographic description of the life of modern Maya in Belize. Thompson also developed a life-long interest in the Colonial documents, which he saw as another portal of entry into the world and mind of the Maya. But, like Morley, Thompson could not resist the challenge of hieroglyphic inscriptions. While Morley's contributions were in recording inscriptions and dating sites, Thompson's were in cataloging the glyphs themselves and trying to improve translation. His two major works were *Maya Hieroglyphic Writing: An Introduction* and *A Catalog of Maya Hieroglyphs*; the latter remains the basic reference for known glyphs. Like Morley, Thompson labored to break the code of non-calendrical glyphs; like Morley, he failed. Thompson's greatest impact was through the books he wrote for a general audience. In charming and witty prose, full of classical and literary allusions, Thompson cast a spell with his version of what the Maya had been. The image, somehow, is very like that of upper-class Anglicans in the novels of Anthony Trollope:

> Perhaps we shall not be too far from reality in regarding the Classic period, mutatis mutandis, as a sort of exotic background for Maya cousins of Archdeacon Grantly, Mrs. Proudie, and Mr. Harding, not in top hats but in quetzal plumes, and sipping not the 1820 port—"it's too good for a bishop, unless one of the right sort"—but the native balche. Indeed, every important Maya ceremonial center might be viewed as a sort of tropical Barchester, and on a mural at Bonampak there is a splendid portrait of Mrs. Proudie watching the bishop at the seat of judgment. Only as long as the right sort were in control did the Classic period endure.

J. Eric S. Thompson was a British archaeologist and epigrapher to whom we owe many discoveries about the Maya calendar and script. His *A Catalog of Maya Hieroglyphs* remains the standard source for identification of glyphs.

The concept of ancient Maya civilization that had grown through the work of Morley and Thompson was brought to general audiences when Morley published *The Ancient Maya*, in 1946, and Thompson produced the first edition of *The Rise and Fall of Maya Civilization*, in 1954. The books were homages to a strange, unworldly people. Pious and devout, at peace with themselves and others, the Maya lived in respectful harmony with nature. They were led by gentle priest-leaders, untutored in the arts of war, whose primary responsibilities were to direct the construction of ever-larger temples and honor the gods with ceremonies. What the leaders did in the worldly realm was not quite clear, because they seemed untroubled by the problems of economy or trade, defense, or power politics that beset rulers in other early civilizations. Thompson pictures Maya rulers as obsessed with the passage of time, counting the slow procession of days in the multiple calendars and commemorating in stone the end of major calendrical periods. Although in the early stages of his career Morley had argued for the probability that hieroglyphic inscriptions recorded history, he had become convinced by the time of *The Ancient Maya* that the still-unreadable passages must be entirely esoteric, full of calendrical and astronomical niceties, and descriptions of gods and ceremonies. Thompson was in full agreement.

Incorporated within this reconstruction of Maya society was the assumption that tropical forest was a very limiting environment that permitted only slash-and-burn farming, the simplest kind of agricultural adaptation. In a slash-and-burn system, vegetation is cut toward the end of the dry season, either in virgin forest or in the secondary growth of a field that has been lying fallow. Once dry, the vegetation is burned; seeds are planted amidst the ashes to await the arrival of the rains. After a couple of years of farming, a plot is left fallow for a number of years to allow the regrowth of native vegetation—a measure to repair damage to the land. If sufficient fallow time is allowed, slash-and-burn farming is productive and sustainable; but because only a small percentage of the land is being farmed at any given time while the rest lies fallow, the system can support only a low population density. Because of this limitation, the great Maya sites had been, in Thompson's view, "vacant ceremonial centers," with only a few priests and specialists in permanent residence. The farmers, meanwhile, lived scattered throughout the countryside near their fields. On days of ceremonies, these country folk thronged to the centers to celebrate great fiestas, then returned, happy and exhausted, to their homes. Peace and harmony permeated Maya life in the Classic period; their society was one that people of today, beset by the hustle and hostility of the 20th century, could envy.

The Classic Maya that Morley and Thompson pictured were unique, not quite like any other people in human history. They seemed too good to be true and, in fact, they were precisely that: the utopian creation of archaeologists extrapolating from scant evidence and led by their own initial presumptions. Although I sometimes regret their passing, these idealized Maya are gone, their image crumbled under a growing weight of archaeological data.

The Carnegie Institution excavations at Uaxactun, Guatemala, were the first to uncover substantial evidence of the Preclassic period. In accord of the day, the investigators treated later levels as expendable and stripped them off to reach the early levels as in this 1937 photo.

with acceptable archaeological practice

3

THE GENESIS OF MAYA CIVILIZATION

The ancestors of the Maya were among the Asian people who trooped across the land bridge that connected Siberia to Alaska some 12,000 or more years ago. They were not yet Maya because the emergence of a recognizable Maya language was still far in the future; the trail of people who were probably Maya begins much later.

By about 2000 B.C., small farming villages formed in the highlands and on the Pacific coast of Guatemala. The domestic plants that would remain the staples of the Mesoamerican diet—corn, squash, and beans—had been borrowed from their places of origin in the semi-arid highlands of Mexico. The pottery so loved by archaeologists had been invented. The earliest villages in the forested lowlands were built later, starting around 1000 B.C. Even at that early date, we can be fairly sure that the inhabitants of the villages both in the highlands and in the lowlands were Maya because there is no evidence from either artifacts or languages that other people ever lived in the area.

Preclassic is the term used today for the period between the first appearance of pottery and the beginning of dated inscriptions in the lowlands—about A.D. 250. Archaeological knowledge of the Preclassic was slow to develop. As recently as the 1930s, summaries of Maya development included statements that now strike us as generic; for example, that there must have been a period of humble villages well before the appearance of the traits referred to as Classic. There was nothing more to say, because nobody had demonstrated the existence of such villages by excavation. Not that interest in early periods was lacking; it was simply that Preclassic levels were deeply buried and hard to investigate. The Maya lived in the same locations for centuries, constantly building larger and larger structures that demolished or buried earlier ones. Hence it was only through massive excavations—requiring a huge investment of time and money—that the early periods could be properly investigated.

The first to tackle the question seriously was the Carnegie Institution project at Uaxactun. A breakthrough occurred at the center of the site, in the major architectural complex known as E Group. Excavations under the plaza revealed deep deposits of pottery that contained none of the painted types

This reconstructed view of Pyramid E-VII sub at Uaxactun, with the stucco masks typical of Preclassic temple architecture, was drawn by Tatiana Proskouriakoff in 1946. Until the beautifully preserved structure was uncovered, archaeologists had not known that monumental architecture existed at such an early date.

marking the Classic period. Such a mass of debris was clearly accumulated over a long period of time, thus implying great antiquity. Next, digging began in Structure E-VII, a large temple platform with four of the earliest stelae at Uaxactun. Excavators trenched through the outer surface—a structure of Early Classic date—hoping to find an earlier building. To their delight, they reached an inner buried structure with a plaster surface in almost pristine condition. As the work progressed, the flanks of the four stairways revealed giant stucco masks, each as remarkably preserved as the plastered walls. A.V. Kidder, Carnegie's director, tells of the impact of the discovery:

> There, snowy white against the deep green wall of the jungle, was a terraced pyramid, perfect in every detail, great stucco masks set on either side of the stairway that mounted to its flat summit, smaller stairways flanking the masks. Directly in front stood a weathered gray stela. It was one of those moments one doesn't forget.

The Carnegie research had opened a new door. This subterranean structure—dubbed E-VII sub—was Preclassic. Not only did it confirm settlement of the lowlands for centuries prior to the Classic period; more significantly, it was clear that the earlier period had known a sophisticated ceremonial structure.

TIKAL AND THE NORTH ACROPOLIS TRENCH

A number of large projects in the 1950s and 1960s were to supply a much better understanding of the Preclassic. One such project was at Tikal—possibly the largest of the Classic sites. There, a University of Pennsylvania team worked

In the first century A.D., this stucco mask was placed on the wall of a structure on Tikal's North Acropolis. Buried a few generations later by new construction, it was discovered in the Tikal Project trench that cut through the acropolis platform.

47

The North Acropolis at Tikal was a huge platform that covered 2.5 acres (1 hectare) and was surmounted by temples. Eleven temples were built on and around the final form of the platform in the Classic period. Buried within the platform were 35 feet (11 meters) of earlier construction.

for 15 years—1956-71—followed by more than 10 years of research by Guatemalan archaeologists. One of the objectives was to learn more about the Preclassic Maya, and Tikal was a likely place to launch the attack. The site was huge and obviously ancient—it had an abundance of Early Classic (A.D. 250-600) stelae, and some of the buildings still standing on the surface were of Early Classic style. I will lean heavily upon the Tikal data; because I worked with the Pennsylvania project for 10 years, Tikal is the site I know best.

Investigating the Preclassic at Tikal was a daunting undertaking. Many of the standing structures rested on giant platforms that covered whatever might be underneath with many feet of construction and fill. Penetrating this mass—even in a single location—would require years of excavation. The place chosen to undertake the task was the North Acropolis that closed the north side of the Great Plaza. Acropolises at Maya sites are complexes that include a number of structures built on a single large platform. The North Acropolis at Tikal stood on a gigantic platform that covered 2.5 acres (1 hectare), and whose most recent floor loomed 35 feet (almost 11 meters) above the level of the Great Plaza. On top and at the front of the Acropolis stood 11 temples, several Early Classic in date, suggesting that the platform was ancient. In order to examine earlier buried levels, a 15-foot (5-meter) trench was cut down until it reached bedrock; the 140-foot-long (43-meter) trench sliced one small temple in half (it was later

This offertory urn is from Burial 85 in Tikal, the tomb of an important man placed in the North Acropolis about A.D. 1. Vessels of this shape occur in burials, but are rarely found in household remains. The dark red slip is characteristic of Late Preclassic ceramics.

reconstructed), and zigzagged around other larger structures to end at the Great Plaza.

The results of the North Acropolis excavations, reported in a six-volume monograph by archaeologist William R. Coe, research director of the Tikal Project, changed forever the image of the lowland Maya Preclassic. As the excavations bore downward, one surprise followed another. The first was that the top five floors of the Classic period, each laid close to the next, constituted but a thin veneer on top of the Acropolis. What really accounted for the platform's height were 12 Preclassic floors, some separated by as much as a dozen feet of stone and earth fill, which had been added to raise the platform to a new height. The remains of early buildings appeared, most of them cut off near the floor to clear for later construction. But one structure, buried almost complete, was wonderfully preserved: Its walls still stood to over seven feet, the stairs flanked by the same sort of plaster masks as were found on E-VII sub at Uaxactun. One tomb emerged, then another, and then a third. The tombs demonstrated beyond question the wealth of the Preclassic elite; long before the beginning of the Classic era, they were ushered into the underworld in splendor. At about 50 B.C., the platform floor of the North Acropolis was ripped open to permit construction of the earliest tomb. In its chamber were placed two bodies, both female. One lay on her back; the second—probably the decayed remains of a seated corpse—was a mere jumble of bones. Jade, a shell necklace, and 20 pottery vessels were included as offerings. The walls of the tomb chamber had been painted red, then covered with a series of figures painted in black. Although the paintings were badly eroded, enough remained to show that they portrayed individuals who had been costumed with all the finery that would mark the upper-class elite in later times. The Maya had already reached a level of social complexity in which some members stood out for their status and possessions.

At about A.D. 1, an important man—probably a king—died. To provide him a resting place, the Maya dug a pit directly in front of what was then the central temple on the Acropolis, and there constructed a vaulted tomb (Burial 85). The body was wrapped in textiles and buried in a seated position. But before the corpse was bundled in its wrappings, the head and upper leg bones had been removed and the severed lower legs placed upside down behind the headless trunk. Such mutilations are fairly common in Maya burials. In fact, we can speculate that in some cases bereaved relatives may have reverently saved pieces of their loved ones to cherish—as recently as the 19th century, the Maya of Belize saved the skulls of departed ancestors and displayed them in their houses. It is also possible, of course, that some of the partial bodies in Maya burials may have been those of war victims, their parts carried off by unfriendly rivals rather than saved by loving relatives. But to return to the tomb of our V.I.P. from A.D. 1, the offerings included a mask of green stone with shell-inlaid eyes—probably to replace the man's absent face. Etched on the forehead of the mask was a headband with the tri-lobed symbol that was the emblem of royalty in Classic times.

This section of the North Acropolis shows the complexity of the architectural sequence that results from the Maya custom of continually building new structures on top of earlier ones. The square tomb just above bedrock near the center contained Burial 85.

Also among the offerings were 26 vessels, including two stately urns that might have been for flowers, and a comic jar in the form of an unidentifiable animal whose tiny snout on one side was opposed by an upright tail that served as the spout. Four of the vessels had been imported from the highlands of Guatemala 200 miles (322 kilometers) away, where rulers at the same time were buried with pottery from the Maya lowlands.

The enormous trench through the North Acropolis at Tikal enabled researchers to see that the Preclassic Maya had reached a much higher level of complexity and sophistication than anyone had anticipated. Centuries of monumental architecture had preceded the Classic period. By the time of Christ, those at the pinnacle of Maya society commanded great wealth, not only to finance the construction of tombs in the most sacred places, but also to stock them with valuables from hundreds of miles away. Even this early, the symbols of royal authority were in place. It is certainly appropriate to speak of kings of Preclassic Tikal, even though they left no inscriptions to tell of their doings.

THE BRIEF FLOURISH AT CERROS

At Tikal, the accomplishments of the Preclassic Maya can be seen only in deep, sunless trenches and dank tunnels. But at a site called Cerros—a more recent project of Southern Methodist University—archaeologist David Freidel has revealed an entire Late Preclassic town that was not buried under tons of later construction and debris. Cerros is in Belize, at the edge of Chetumal Bay—a large inlet from the Caribbean. Near Cerros, the New River empties into the bay, so the town is in an ideal location to reap the resources of bay and river, and to deal with coastal trade bound upriver from the ocean. At about 50

The partially excavated temple at Cerros, Belize, shows two of the four masks that flanked the stairway.

B.C., Cerros was only a cluster of pole-and-thatch huts near the water's edge, a simple fishing village as it had been for several centuries. Then, a great ceremony took place. A section of houses was leveled and covered with earth. Dishes from a ritual feast were broken, then scattered about; precious pieces of jade were crushed and added to the offerings, along with water lilies and the flowers of fruit trees. Once the area had been thus cleared and sanctified, construction began. A masonry temple of three rooms was built atop a steep, two-tiered pyramid. Four giant tree trunks were set up inside the temple rooms, symbols, Freidel believes, of the mythical trees the Maya thought held up the corners of the universe. Finally, four giant stucco masks—as at Uaxactun and Tikal—flanked the single stairway that rose to the temple. The masks formed a cosmological map. The bottom two, on the first tier of the pyramid, were snarling jaguar faces representing the Sun God—the rising sun to the east and setting sun to the west. Above them were masks of Venus—the morning star and evening star—hovering above the sun as they do in the sky. What rites took place in the temple we cannot know. Our best guess is that they may have insured the continued daily rise and fall of the sun, and the continued growth and replenishment of human beings and of corn.

This first temple at Cerros was not to stand alone for long. Soon a second, much larger, temple was erected, nearly in front of the first; this was followed by a third, then a fourth temple, each endowed with complex celestial imagery. Yet hardly was this spate of construction completed than it was terminated with a ritual not unlike the one that had initiated the whole cycle. Great fires were banked against the masks and a feast was followed by the smashing of vessels. Once more jade was pounded to bits—and then the center of Cerros was abandoned. For reasons we will never know, the people departed and the site lay empty.

The site of Nakbe in far northern Guatemala had pyramids as tall as 135 feet (45 meters), some of which were constructed as early as 600 B.C. Here, a partially cleared pyramid at the site shows fragments of still-standing stone walls and a stairway.

EL MIRADOR AND NAKBE

The greatest surprise about the Preclassic Maya lay far to the north in Guatemala, near the Mexican border. It was a site called El Mirador that had been visited and briefly described in the 1930s. Despite the fact that the largest temples protrude above the forest like those at Tikal—they were clearly visible in the distance as planes approached the most northerly airstrip in Guatemala—the site was rarely mentioned; nobody had tried to revisit it for years. Strangely, El Mirador yielded no stelae, despite its size (although a few fragmentary ones have been found there since), and generated little interest in those inscription-hunting days. Also offputting was El Mirador's location. The northwest corner of Guatemala is a forbidding spot. Surrounded by huge seasonal swamps, impassable in the rainy season and damp and unpleasant even in the dry, the site is far from roads and trails (even today, El Mirador is still three days by foot or mule from the last settlement in northern Guatemala). In the 1960s, Ian Graham, of the Peabody Museum at Harvard, decided to visit El Mirador. Despite his experience in the forest (he is the foremost living expert in discovering sites and recording inscriptions), it took him weeks to find the site. To those unfamiliar with virgin forest, it may seem strange that pyramids visible from the air could be lost. But the vegetation is so dense that a 200-foot-high (61-meter-high) pyramid cannot be seen from the ground if one passes less than than 20 yards (18 meters) from its base. Graham's report of the size of the rediscovered site stirred interest anew and led to preliminary archaeological investigations that began in the late 1970s.

The results were unexpected, to say the least. Not only did the largest structural complexes at El Mirador dwarf those of Tikal, but they were constructed entirely in the Preclassic! And for sheer size, El Mirador is staggering. More than a dozen temple pyramids and complexes soar skyward. At the tallest, El Tigre pyramid, a temple 180 feet (55 meters) high greets the rising sun. The Central Acropolis, itself more than 300 yards (274 meters) long, is a vast complex of buildings that probably served as the city's headquarters. Then, half a mile east of the central section stands the Danta Complex, another huge cluster of buildings centered upon a giant pyramid, on top of which sits a great temple flanked by two smaller ones. Located on a hill above the central area, the Danta Complex—at 230 feet (70 meters) the tallest Maya construction known—looms over the rest of the site. Its scale is immense. If the complex were placed on top of the Great Plaza at Tikal, not only would it cover the plaza and Temples I, II, and III, but it also would obliterate the entire North Acropolis. Causeways—still easily visible from the air—run for miles from El Mirador, crossing the great swamps surrounding the site and continuing outward to still-unknown locations. Hordes of laborers must have been involved in the construction of El Mirador, yet the site remains too little investigated to permit population estimates—or even to speculate why the Maya chose to locate their greatest early site in this swampy, woebegone area. Nor is it known what still-earlier buildings lie hidden in the depths of construction beneath the final complexes.

Another surprise was forthcoming when UCLA archaeologist Richard Hansen began work at the neighboring site of Nakbe in the late 1980s. Nakbe, 10 miles (16 kilometers) southeast of El Mirador, is not so large as its giant neighbor, but is still a respectable site, with major pyramids 135 feet (45 meters) high. Hansen hoped that it might date to the Preclassic as well, and that it perhaps had been a satellite of El Mirador. It proved to be Preclassic, indeed; in fact, Nakbe was even more ancient, with its major structures dating back as far as 600 B.C.

PARALLEL PATHS TO CIVILIZATION

Discoveries of older and older sites have pushed back the beginning of Maya civilization ever further in time, transforming our understanding both of the lowland Maya and of their relationship to other civilizations. One result has been to destroy a once-popular theory that Olmec civilization—located on the gulf coast of Mexico—provided the seed of Maya civilization.

The Olmec, who, like the Maya, lived in a tropical forest environment, had created a spectacular art style by 1200 B.C. Giant stone heads, some of them 9 feet (3 meters) high, were the most eye-catching pieces. But equally splendid in their own way were delicate jadeite figurines, often depicting human individuals with the snarling mouths and pointed fangs of jaguars. Only two Olmec sites have been thoroughly investigated by archaeologists. San Lorenzo, in the state of Veracruz, Mexico, is not a big site by the standards of later periods; it contains only a few architectural structures, none very large. But an abundance of sculpture occurs at San Lorenzo, and the date—1200 to 900 B.C.—is early. The second excavated Olmec site is La Venta, located on the Tonala River, 18 miles (29 kilometers) inland from the Gulf of Mexico. La Venta is larger than San Lorenzo, with one mound that is 100 feet (30 meters) high. The major structures here date between 800 and 400 B.C., by which time the art style featured low-relief carvings portraying rulers and ceremonial scenes. Some of the carvings bear a resemblance to later Classic Maya stelae, using symbols that are probably the progenitors of Maya hieroglyphs.

When Olmec sites were first dated by radiocarbon in the 1950s and 1960s, the archaeological profession was dumbfounded, especially at the 1200 B.C. date of San Lorenzo. The San Lorenzo sculpture was far more sophisticated than anything known elsewhere in Mesoamerica at such an early date. It seemed possible that Olmec was the mother-culture for all of Mesoamerica and that, like civilizational Johnny Appleseeds, the Olmec had wandered hither and yon planting the ideas of civilization. More recently, archaeological research has shown that by 1200 B.C. a number of areas in Mesoamerica had already taken the first steps to complexity on their own, and that the Olmec—notwithstanding the wide impact of their well-developed art—were only one of a number of early civilizations. The discovery of Nakbe changes the situation still further. Nakbe dwarfs La Venta, leaving little doubt that by 600 B.C. the Maya had outstripped the Olmec in size of centers and architectural development.

It now seems unlikely that the social complexity of ancient Mesoamerica originated from a single source; rather, a number of peoples probably embarked upon parallel paths toward civilization in several different places, including the Maya area. As population grew, some individuals in these societies accumulated wealth and power, and emerged as an upper class. Ritual became more elaborate, and was expressed in increasingly sophisticated art and in settings requiring special buildings. Economic specialization became more important, both in the production of utilitarian items that could be made in specialized centers more efficiently than in individual households and in the creation of unique items that would distinguish the rising elite from lesser people. Interest in rare and valuable materials such as jade stimulated trade and contact between different areas, whose leaders learned from each other, borrowing both goods and ideas.

The Maya were one of the peoples who underwent this growth process, inventing and borrowing to create the distinctive blend that was Maya civilization. But the specifics of this general process in the Maya area remain foggy. Much more information about El Mirador and Nakbe is badly needed, particularly about what preceded the complicated sites that emerged as the final products. In addition, we need to know more about the earliest development at such sites as Tikal. More surprises undoubtedly still wait to be unearthed.

The most striking artifacts of the Olmec civilization were colossal stone heads, most of which seem to date between 1200 and 900 B.C. These heads are now believed to be portraits of Olmec leaders.

54

From the air, Palenque still retains much of its splendor. First discovered in 1746 by a Spanish priest who stumbled across "stone houses" while remained one of the best-preserved Maya sites. The large complex near the center is the Palace; to the right, is the Temple of the Inscriptions.

4

THE CLASSIC IN FULL FLOWER

Because of our image of classical antiquity, the word "Classic" implies the heights of cultured accomplishment. In a Classic period, we envision musicians filling the streets with celestial harmonies, poets praising the universe under arches designed by the greatest architects who ever lived. And this is the image Mayanists had in mind when they adopted the term Classic in the 1950s. The period in question was set by inscriptions dated in the Maya calendar. At around A.D. 300 in our calendar, the first inscriptions

looking for new land to cultivate, Palenque has

appeared in Maya sites. There were no awkward preliminary attempts. Even the earliest were beautiful—it was as though the gods had delivered them complete. Then, after 600 years, they ceased. These dated inscriptions occurred at the largest of lowland sites, the ones with the most impressive architecture, the most remote and mysterious. The sites and the period indeed seemed "Classic"—the Maya had been at their best. If the calendar had burst forth full-blown, without visible preliminary stages, it seemed possible that all the wonders thought to mark the Classic period had similarly appeared completely and suddenly—like a rabbit from a magician's hat.

Yet, as archaeological research revealed the centuries of Preclassic development, the impression of a mysterious burst of civilization at a single moment disappeared. Clearly, the distinctive traits of Maya architecture had developed gradually—and hundreds of years earlier than once thought. Other developments also considered "Classic," kings and royal burials, for example, were found to have occurred equally early. Little was left to make A.D. 300 a watershed, except the birth of the custom of erecting carved and dated monuments and placing them in key locations at the centers of sites.

The term Classic endures, but now it is no more than a chronological label for the period of dated inscriptions between A.D. 250 (monuments predating 300 have since been discovered) and 950. The chronology has become more precise, with the period now divided into three sections: an Early Classic from 250 to 600; a Late Classic from 600 to 830; and a newly recognized Terminal Classic from 830 to 950—an era when most southern lowland sites were in the throes of collapse. Most of the sites in the southern Maya lowlands are referred to as Classic; while some may also have been occupied during the Preclassic era, they were invariably abandoned at the end of the Terminal Classic and never reoccupied.

CLASSIC MAYA SITES

A visitor's initial impression of a Classic Maya site is of open spaces and large stone buildings. The buildings appear unexpectedly, especially if the area has not been cleared of forest. Some of the buildings seem isolated, while others occur in clusters. One clambers up and down endlessly. A breathless climb to the top of a platform covered by buildings may be followed by a slippery descent to a low area that seems devoid of any construction. The hardy may scramble up a frightening slope, clutching trees or bushes as handholds, to stand in the doorway of a temple; from there, other temples can be seen, rising from the forest.

Maya sites seem to adhere to no obvious plan—there are no grids of streets or blocks laid out at right angles. But there is, in fact, a plan that makes all Maya cities much alike in basic layout. Every large site consists of a series of architectural groups—often separated from each other by as much as half a mile—linked by broad paved causeways. In each group, the structures are arranged around open plazas, now often grassy or overgrown with tropical vegetation. In Maya times they were paved with dazzling white plaster that sparkled in the tropical sunlight. One plaza is usually recognizable as the most important because it contains the greatest number of stone carvings and is surrounded by the largest buildings. Temples tower above the main plaza, some solitary on giant pyramids, others whole groups that are clustered on a large platform. At one side of the plaza is a jumble of low stone buildings and courtyards, entered only by narrow passageways; these obviously were not meant for public traverse. Upright stone slabs called stelae, accompanied by round slabs called altars (perhaps mistakenly, because they simply may have been daises for public pronouncements), stand in rows in front of temples. The carvings on the stelae most frequently show a single standing figure whose ornate costume fills the surrounding space. At the edges of the figure, or on the sides of the stelae, hieroglyphic inscriptions relate history.

What makes Maya sites so impressive is their wonderful stone buildings. The labor invested in their construction is beyond comprehension. Crowds of humble peasants must have quarried stone from the limestone bedrock, then carried it to construction sites; others, meanwhile, amassed piles of wood to feed the fires that transformed limestone into mortar and plaster. Then there must have been hordes of more specialized workers: masons, plasterers, carvers (at sites with decorated facades), as well as architects to design it all.

Maya architects labored under a severe handicap: They never discovered the principle of the true arch, whose distribution of weight makes possible the soaring ceilings of Gothic cathedrals. Instead, the Maya roofed their structures using the corbeled arch, a crude technique with major limitations. This is the same method used by children to make houses from blocks. At the top of a wall, each additional block is made to project inward just a bit—not enough to topple the wall—toward a corresponding wall on the other side of an open space. Little by little, the walls on each side approach each other, and a closure is finally achieved. The technique worked poorly when we were children—our make-believe houses usually collapsed when we tried to put the final block on top. The technique worked poorly for the Maya, too. The only force able to keep each stone from tumbling into a room is a counterbalancing weight on its non-projecting end. The result is massive walls—and narrow rooms; Maya walls are often so close together that a person's outstretched arms can touch both sidewalls at once.

On the exteriors, however, Maya architects were capable of magnificent effects. Angles and overhangs, inset corners and projecting moldings—a whole series of tricks were used to play with light and shadow. The impact of a reconstructed Maya building in the tropical sunlight is breathtaking.

The two most common stone structures are "temples" and "palaces." The temples sit upon pyramid-shaped substructures, usually a stack of several terraces of decreasing size. The pyramids reach fearful heights, very often more

The Great Plaza of Tikal, exhibiting all the features of Classic architecture and site planning, is surrounded by the city's largest and most important buildings. The Central Acropolis, where the Tikal rulers probably lived, and Temple V are in the middle of this photo, with Temple I to the left and Temple II to the right. The stelae and altars that characterize main plazas appear in the foreground.

than 100 feet (30 meters), the equivalent of a 10-story building today; some exceed 150 feet (46 meters). Dizzying stairways sweep up the front, their steps too narrow for anything more than the ball of the foot—a misstep means an uninterrupted plunge to the plaza below. Maya priests and dignitaries climbed these awful steps weighed down with unwieldy costumes and laden with gifts for the gods (and presumably praying with all their might). Some archaeologists believe that prisoners were sacrificed by being trussed up like balls, then thrown down the stairways so that they would bounce unhindered to the plazas below. The pyramids beneath the temples are solid (usually most of the mass consists of earlier buildings covered over), with no interior rooms or passageways, although they usually hide sealed tombs. Even the temples on top contain only a few narrow rooms, unlit except for whatever light comes in the doorways. These rooms are dark and secret, places suited to hushed ceremonies

60

rather than throngs and hymns. Above the temple, purely decorative roof-combs enhance the effect of verticality, and often served as frameworks for giant stucco figures.

That temples were, in fact, religious buildings is beyond question; structures of the same shape were still in use when the Spaniards arrived and described with horror the bloody sacrifices that took place within the temple walls. Palaces are quite different, having a purely secular use—and an entirely dissimilar construction. Resting on low platforms rather than on pyramids, Maya palaces have multiple doorways and suites of interconnected rooms. In some rooms, plaster-and-stone thrones look through doorways onto courtyards where one can easily envision crowds of supplicants. Other rooms are encircled by benches that may have been used as sleeping spaces; curtain-rod holders set into doorjambs suggest a desire for privacy. It seems likely that palaces were

Sculpture, either in stone or in modeled plaster, was an integral part of Maya architecture. Among the most famous examples is the Hieroglyphic Stairway at Copan where the modeled figures stand out from the text carved on the stairway risers.

home to the uppermost elite, but the variety of the rooms and their arrangement suggest additional functions—administration, perhaps, or as storage rooms for valuables.

Ball courts are a third kind of structural complex found near the centers of sites. Sixteenth-century accounts refer to a ball game played at that time, and Classic period art depicts games in progress. The game was intimately connected to religion and sacrifice, but the rules of play are unclear. The ball used in the Classic period was huge—more than a foot in diameter. It was struck with the thigh, torso, shoulders, or upper arms, but not with the hands or feet. Players wore knee and elbow pads and a bulky waist protector called a yoke, which was probably fashioned from hides or wood.

The court consisted of two parallel platforms with sloping sides outlining a narrow playing alley that expanded into two end zones, making an "I" shape. Some ball courts were equipped with stone rings—through which the ball

The Ball Court at Copan lies near the foot of the hieroglyphic stairway. These courts were symbolic of the boundaries between the actual and supernatural worlds. Maya ball games were intimately related to ritual, death, and sacrifice, and there is little doubt that, at least on some occasions, losing players were sacrificed.

passed—at the sides of the playing alley. Also, at the sides or ends above some courts were small stone buildings, thought to have been used for dressing, equipment storage, or ceremonies.

The central plaza and its structures are only the beginning, for in a major Maya site, stone buildings number in the hundreds. Additional plazas—almost as grand as the central one—are adjoined to it by causeways; these raised roadways are wide enough, as the Spaniards said, for 10 horsemen abreast. But the Maya had neither horses nor wheeled vehicles, and it seems likely that the causeways were designed for ceremonial processions, a custom still at the center of the surviving religious practices of the Maya today. One could hardly, after all, imagine rulers—arrayed like those depicted on stelae—sloshing through the mud to reach another temple. As one moves outward from the center of a Maya site, the stone structures become smaller. Within sites, and then in the surrounding countryside, a new cluster of temples and palaces appears every half mile or so, presumably to serve as secondary centers for local religious and administrative purposes.

RETHINKING THE NUMBERS

Scattered between the ceremonial and elite structures were the houses of the lower classes. Archaeological research before World War II paid little attention to small structures. Temples and palaces, tombs and carvings had been too attractive. But for archaeologists whose training is in anthropology, the main goal is finding out how people lived—*all* people, not just the rich and famous. In 1940 and 1948 respectively, Clyde Kluckhohn, a cultural anthropologist, then Walter Taylor, a young archaeologist, had attacked Maya archaeology for its "tombs-and-temples" mentality. Archaeology, they said, had been too anti-quarian, concerned with beautiful buildings and objects to the exclusion of people. Kluckhohn called it "archaeology at the intellectual level of stamp collecting." Bitter pill though it was, there was truth in the criticisms: Maya archaeologists had indeed walked into sites with their eyes cast skyward, on the hunt for the tallest temple, which they then attacked with remarkable vigor.

As archaeological activity resumed after World War II, new research directions were in order. For example, when the Carnegie Institution reassembled its team and excavated Mayapan—a Late Postclassic site, far less spectacular than such earlier targets as Chichen Itza and Uaxactun—a new part of the research was a map of the whole site, rather than just the central ceremonial precinct. The new people-oriented approach started to catch on. Gordon Willey, newly appointed to the prestigious position of Bowditch Professor of Archaeology at Harvard, chose as his first Maya project Barton Ramie, a small site in Belize that had not a single pyramid. His first step: to dig small platforms and map the site. And when the Tikal Project began its work in 1956, one of its objectives was to map all structures within a 6.2-square-mile (16-square-kilometer) area centered on the Great Plaza.

The results were quite remarkable. Once the researchers' eyes were turned downward, they found scores of small mounds 2 or 3 feet (.75 meter to 1 meter) high and 20 to 30 feet (6 to 9 meters) in length. To the uninitiated, these mounds can easily pass for natural bumps in the ground surface, but careful inspection reveals lines of stone that are clearly not the work of nature. Excavation shows that the mounds are the remains of small, stone-walled platforms, each housing a wealth of debris—fragments of pottery, broken stone tools, stones for grinding corn. Centuries ago, the platform floors were finished in plaster, enough of which remains to show holes left by long-disintegrated wooden posts. The platforms were, in fact, bases for the same pole-and-thatch houses that fill Maya villages today. Cool and comfortable in the moist tropics, they have remained unchanged for millennia. All necessary materials are available in the forest, and a crew of workers can construct a house in a couple of days.

When completed, the Tikal site map showed more than 3000 structures, most of them house platforms. In 1965, William Haviland, in charge of small-structure research at Tikal, made a first estimate of the population in the Tikal

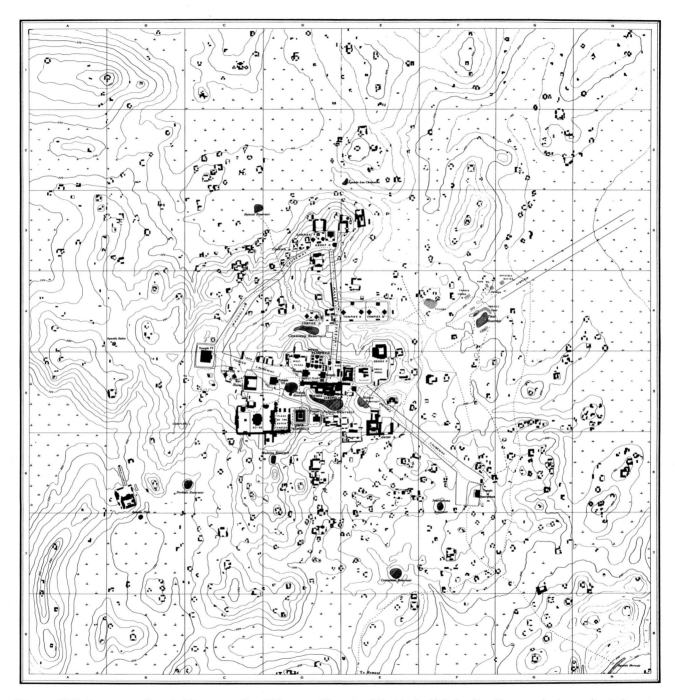

"Greater" Tikal—an area of nearly 50 square miles (120 square kilometers) that had a high density of houses—had an estimated population of 62,000 at its peak in the Late Classic period. Within the six square miles (16 square kilometers) shown here, the population was likely about 15,000. Raised causeways radiate from the central Great Plaza. Each small black rectangle is a house platform.

mapped area: 11,000 people. The estimate raised a storm of controversy. Until that point, Maya sites had been considered vacant ceremonial centers with only a few hundred inhabitants; besides, this was far more people than could have been supported by simple slash-and-burn farming (then considered the only system possible in tropical forest). Haviland's Tikal population figure was obviously a major challenge to the traditional conception of Maya society. The debate stimulated maps and mound-counts at other sites, with results that substantiated the unexpectedly high population density.

There is no denying that thousands of people lived in the Maya lowland centers. True, the cities' central sectors were not particularly heavily populated, but residences continued far into the surrounding countryside, and there were no large unpopulated areas between one center and the next. By the time the Tikal Project had finished its work, it had been discovered that what might be called "Greater Tikal" covered an area of nearly 50 square miles (120 square kilometers) and contained 62,000 people. Today, site maps and population estimates from a large number of sites in the southern lowlands indicate an average population density of more than 500 people per square mile (200 per square kilometer) at the peak of the Late Classic. To put it in perspective, this density is matched only by the most heavily populated areas of the world, such as the Indonesian island of Java or the densest parts of China.

FEEDING THE POPULATION

Once the exceedingly high population of the Maya lowlands became evident, archaeologists had to face the question of how so many people had been fed. Even the most efficient slash-and-burn farming could sustain less than half the number of people who lived in the lowlands. There are, however, alternatives that could provide food for greater numbers. The lengthy fallow cycles of slash-and-burn farming might be shortened, the land refarmed before it was rested. Each field would yield somewhat less this way than with a full fallow cycle, but the increased amount of land available for cultivation might offset the loss. In addition, large sections of the lowlands have a long enough rainy season to permit two crops each year. The second crop is a risky one; some years it will be good, some years the rains will stop early, leaving it a total loss. But again, there will be an average increase in food production.

When archaeologists turned their attention to farming systems, they found evidence of more intensive agricultural techniques. In several parts of the lowlands, terraces were discovered on the sloping sides of ridges; these would have prevented erosion and helped to hold plant nutrients and water. Then, seasonal and permanent swamps in several parts of the lowlands were found to contain agricultural features. In wetlands that had been cleared, aerial photos showed patterns of fields surrounded by canals. Such canals either would have raised fields above the water or served to drain water at the end of the rainy season to prepare the swampy areas for a dry-season crop. Because wet-

The maize god—depicted in this statue from Uxmal as a handsome young man with maize foliage as a headdress—figures prominently in Maya art.

Slash-and-burn agriculture is still common among Maya farmers today. Although the system is ecologically sound and easy, it can support only a low population density. It is now clear that the Maya used many other agricultural methods in addition to slash-and-burn farming.

lands cover as much as half the land surface in some parts of the lowlands, their use would drastically increase food production. All in all, archaeologists now agree (though they argue bitterly about details) that Maya agriculture in times of peak population must have been far more intensive than anybody had guessed. Ancient pollen samples show that the forest was almost completely cut; the samples show pollen from crops, weeds, and secondary growth—but very little from mature trees. One can envision almost complete utilization of the land, the Maya harvesting crops on ridges during the rainy season, and in wetland fields during the dry. The fields must have been crammed with workers, laboring from dawn till dusk.

In effect, traditional assumptions about population and agriculture have been turned upside down. The Classic Maya were not, in fact, a low-density population living from a very conservative system of farming, but were instead one of the world's densest populations, supporting themselves by a desperately intensive agricultural system designed to coax maximum production from the environment.

On the back wall of Tikal's Temple of the Inscriptions is a very long hieroglyphic text carved in 766. Badly eroded, the inscription is difficult to than 1000 years before the date of the carving. They may refer to real or mythical ancestors of the Tikal rulers.

5

HIGH SOCIETY

At about the same time that research was devastating old ideas about Maya population and agriculture in the rain forest, a second long-held concept fell: The sudden and stunning decipherment of Maya hieroglyphic writing dealt a deathblow to the image of the gentle priest-leader. The interpretation of the calendrical and astronomical segments of inscriptions had been a brilliant achievement of late 19th-century scholarship. But after that, progress with the non-calendrical glyphs had been

The Tikal emblem glyph shows the characteristic features of this class of glyphs. The two glyphs (Ben and Ich) at the top read "Lord"; the "water prefix" at the front is thought to represent blood and the large main sign to the lower right is the identifier of Tikal. The whole emblem glyph, then, reads "Blood Lord of Tikal" and is, in fact, the title of a noble from the site.

almost nonexistent for more than 50 years. Because the non-calendrical inscriptions proved so intractable, the impression gradually grew that they must deal entirely with complicated esoterica concerned with gods, ceremonies, and cosmology. Having repeatedly insisted, in the early stages of his career, that the inscriptions contained historical sections, Sylvanus Morley had reversed his position by 1946, when he vehemently denied that there was any such information:

> The Maya inscriptions treat primarily of chronology, astronomy...and religious matters. They are in no sense records of personal glorification and self-laudation like the inscriptions of Egypt, Assyria, and Babylonia. They tell no story of kingly conquests, recount no deeds of imperial achievement; they neither praise nor exalt, glorify nor aggrandize, indeed they are so utterly impersonal, so completely nonindividualistic, that it is even probable that the name-glyphs of specific men and women were never recorded upon the Maya monuments.

The first hint that this prevailing wisdom might be mistaken came in 1958 when Heinrich Berlin, a German epigrapher, published a paper on what he called "emblem glyphs." Berlin had noticed a pattern of a particular glyph block (the squarish units, each containing several glyphs, that are the building blocks of Maya inscriptions). At site after site across the lowlands this glyph block invariably featured two glyphs at the top—*ben* and *ich*—and at the front had a preliminary string of dots called the "water prefix." The combination of

At the front of this inscription is the emblem glyph of Copan, the main sign of which depicts a leaf-nosed bat. The long nose of the bat in other carvings sometimes looks like the trunk of an elephant and in earlier days created speculations about connections with Asia.

ben-ich and water prefix, identical at every site, surrounded a "main sign" that occupied the rest of the glyph block. These main signs differed from one site to the next. At Tikal, the main sign looked like a bundle of reeds bent and tied with a cord; at Copan, it portrayed the head of a fruit-eating bat. It seemed likely to Berlin that these emblem glyphs represented the names of sites, or perhaps the names of their dynasties. If this was true, the writing was at least worldly enough to permit the Maya to name their sites.

Two years later, in 1960, Mayanists were stunned by an article published by Tatiana Proskouriakoff, a quiet, unassuming woman and brilliant scholar, who had been working with the glyphs. Proskouriakoff, born in Siberia, had come to the United States as a child. With a degree in architecture from Pennsylvania State University, she entered the world of Maya archaeology as an illustrator. She was invited to assist the University of Pennsylvania Project at Piedras Negras in 1936, then went on to work with most of the Carnegie Institution's major projects. An exceedingly skilled artist, she produced *An Album of Maya Architecture* in 1946—a popular work that recreates the feeling of Maya sites so well that it is still in print today. With an intellectual skill that matched her draftsmanship, she published *A Study of Classic Maya Sculpture* in 1950; this masterpiece provides a still-used system to date Maya sculptures on the basis of features such as details of costume.

Then came Proskouriakoff's tour de force. A 1960 article, prosaically entitled "Historical Implications of a Pattern of Dates at Piedras Negras, Guatemala," established in a single stroke that Maya inscriptions dealt with history. Although Proskouriakoff was fastidious about crediting a comprehensive list of previous researchers for ideas that helped stimulate her accomplishment, the discovery was almost entirely her own, brilliantly demonstrated in a mere 21 pages. Remarkably, Proskouriakoff's exposition was so convincing that not a single voice was raised in protest—unlike many scholarly revolutions that are argued bitterly for years before acceptance. J. Eric S. Thompson, for example, having rigorously inveighed against historicity in Maya writing, graciously capitulated: "[This] work has shown that the generally held view, to which I subscribed...regarding the impersonality of the texts is completely mistaken."

Proskouriakoff's breakthrough was a remarkably simple one, based upon a collation of scenes and dates on Piedras Negras stelae. The stelae at the site occur in sets found at different locations; the dates within each set are clustered and differ from the dates in other sets. Proskouriakoff noticed that the first stela in each set showed a similar scene of an individual seated in a niche, with a ladder and, sometimes, footprints leading up to the niche. A sacrificial victim was often found at the base of the ladder. Thompson had explained the scene as showing "gods seated in niches formed by the bodies of celestial dragons"; and at first Proskouriakoff also attempted a religious explanation:

Tatiana Proskouriakoff, seen at work here in 1978, entered Maya archaeology as an illustrator. Her brilliant demonstration that Maya glyphs told of history was one of the most important discoveries of this century.

Tatiana Proskouriakoff rendered restorations of single buildings and parts of ancient Maya cities. Her subjects were shown in perspective, plotted from the most accurate measurements available. This is a reconstruction of Structure 1 from Xpuhil in Campeche, Mexico, where the three towers were not real temples, but solid masonry that appears to have no functional use other than to break the severely rectangular contour.

My first thought was that the 'niche' motif represented the dedication of a new temple, and that the ladder ascending to the niche marked with footsteps symbolized the rise to the sky of the victim of sacrifice, whose body was sometimes shown at the foot of the ladder. It occurred to me that if I searched the inscriptions for a hieroglyph peculiar to these stelae, I might find the glyphic expression for human sacrifice. What I found instead started an entirely new train of thought and led to surprising conclusions.

The "ascension motif," as Proskouriakoff called the scene with the niche, had a date that was clearly important because it was referred to in the inscriptions of other stelae in the same set. Also invariably used when this date was mentioned was the "toothache glyph," so named because it shows the head of a bird whose head is bound with a rag that passes underneath the beak and ends in a bow atop the head—just like an ancient toothache remedy. After a set of stelae had run its course, a new set began, initiated again by a stela with an ascension motif and a new date marked by the toothache glyph. In addition, Proskouriakoff discovered that:

> ...it is not the "toothache glyph" date that is the earliest in each set, but another that is anywhere from twelve to thirty-one years earlier and is always accompanied by the so-called "upended frog glyph." This earlier event could not have had much public importance when it happened since no notation was made of it at the time. It was first recorded after the "toothache glyph" event occurred, and only then began to be celebrated by anniversaries.

> Doubtless there are various events in history that are paired in this way, but surely the most common is the birth of some person who in his mature years acquires great prestige or political power...

> The next step, of course, was to identify the names of the lords, or at least to make sure that the birth and accession date referred to the same individual. If so, the "upended frog glyph" (birth date), and the "toothache glyph" (accession) of each set of records would be followed by the same glyph, which would differ for every set. This actually proved to be the case, though the name was expressed by three or four glyphs....

Proskouriakoff discovered, when studying the stelae at Piedras Negras, that the birthday or "upended frog" glyph *(top)* referred to birth or some other event early in the life of an individual, while the "toothache" glyph *(below)* meant accession.

Here, then, was history, and the conclusion was strengthened by the fact that the span of time covered by any single set of stelae was never more than 64 years, a plausible interval for a human life.

Needless to say, Proskouriakoff's discovery does not involve reading a glyph in ancient Maya, but simply recognizing its meaning. Whether or not any of the Maya glyphs were phonetic—representing sounds—had been debated for years. After the failure of Landa's "alphabet" to produce anything meaningful, however, relatively few scholars had attempted phonetic approaches. The breakthrough in this aspect of decipherment came in the mid 1950s from Yuri Knorozov, a young Soviet researcher who had never even visited a Maya site.

Recognizing that Landa's list was not a true alphabet, Knorozov hypothesized that it might be a syllabary—in which each sign stands for a combination of consonant and vowel. He achieved some viable readings of the codices, but unlike Proskouriakoff's discovery, Knorozov's work was bitterly debated; it was several years before its correctness was generally recognized by all scholars. It is now clear that Maya hieroglyphic writing is a mixed script. Some signs are syllabic, while many others are logograms, in which the glyph stands for an entire word or concept, and has no phonetic reading. Among the phonetic glyphs, those for about half of the possible syllables from the Maya language have been recognized, and an increasing number of linguistic readings in ancient Maya are available.

In the years following these breakthroughs, the decipherments moved slowly, unveiling only a few events in the lives of rulers. Then, as glyphs were

THE NAMES OF THE ANCIENT MAYA

What is the origin of the wonderful names—Bird Jaguar, Stormy Sky, Smoking Frog—that epigraphers give to the ancient Maya? And are they what the Maya actually called themselves? There are several ways of taking name glyphs from the inscriptions and creating equivalents we can use in English. One way is simply to describe what the name glyph looks like: Bird Jaguar, for instance, is so called because his name glyph features a bird sitting on the head of a jaguar. Alternatively, one can use Maya words to describe the glyphs: Chan Bahlum is Maya for Snake Jaguar. Or else, one can use a combination of Maya and English words: The ruler

**Yaxun Balam
(Bird Jaguar)**

Kan Boar, at Tikal, has a name glyph that combines the head of a peccary and the Maya Kan Cross (a glyph, resembling a St. Andrew's cross, for one of the named days in the Maya 260-day calendar). A few rulers' names actually can be read phonetically. For example, the ruler whose real name in Maya is most secure is Pacal of

**Chan Bahlum
(Snake Jaguar)**

Palenque. The common form of his name glyph shows a round object that seems to be a shield, so in some early articles he was called "Lord Shield." A second way in which his name is written uses three separate glyphs representing the Maya syllables "pa," "ca," and "la"—pacala. Consulting 16th-century Maya-Spanish dictionaries for the word "pacal" (the "a" of the last syllable "la" is silent), one discovers that "pacal" in Maya means "shield." So Pacal was the ruler's name, and the Maya left no doubt about it.

Would they had been so helpful with other rulers, because, to be frank, the process of naming rulers is completely out of control. Whoever discovers the name of a ruler is free to read

and publish it as he or she wishes; but whoever else reads the same inscriptions is free to change the name if a better reading suggests itself. As a result, the 16th ruler of Copan has been called variously Yax Pac, Yax Sun-at-Horizon, New Sun-at-

**Yax Pac
(Sun-at-Horizon)**

Horizon, Rising Sun, Madrugada (Spanish for dawn), and First Dawn. Fearful of such profusion of names, some epigraphers choose simply to give numbers to rulers at a site: for example, Rulers 1, 2, 3, and 4 of Dos Pilas. Because I lack the skill to impose order upon chaos, I have chosen in this volume the simple expedient of using whichever commonly used name seems easiest to understand.

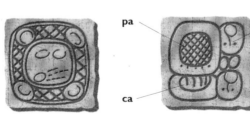

pa   la

ca

Pacal (Lord Shield)

interpreted one by one, the pace of decipherment escalated until a veritable flood of information was added to the store each year. Today, if a new Classic period inscription is discovered, about 90 percent of it can be read within a few days and only 10 percent remains puzzling. Epigraphers estimate that as much as 50 percent of the available corpus of Classic period inscriptions has already been read.

What *are* the long-awaited messages in Maya hieroglyphic inscriptions? Before the code, as it were, was cracked, one might have hoped that the inscriptions contained great literature, or philosophy, or the Maya understanding of science. None of these matters, in fact, are there, nor are the more mundane concerns of bookkeepers or tax collectors. Instead, the inscriptions contain royal records—bare-bones documentation telling of kings and, sometimes, queens. Dates of births, deaths, inaugurations, occasionally the names of parents, defeated enemies, important ceremonies, political events—these are the details that unfold before us. Much of Maya life is quite untouched by the Classic period writings, and too little remains undeciphered to hold any hope that major new categories of information await discovery. It is very likely that libraries of books written on paper held such information as tribute lists, inventories of royal storehouses—even literary masterpieces. But if such libraries existed, they are gone forever; no imaginable trick of preservation would have protected them from the ravages of centuries of tropical heat and humidity.

These real Maya, whose stories can now be read, are vastly different from the gentle priest-philosophers imagined by Eric Thompson. The real rulers exult in the thrill of battle; blood-soaked and elated, they delight in the torture of their captives. The self-aggrandizement that Sylvanus Morley could not imagine within the scope of Maya temperament rings in almost every line. Royal accomplishments are always grand; everything is always well, with never a hint of trouble. Kings liken themselves to the gods. They personally perform all ceremonies, they fight all battles. They were, in a word, egomaniacs (a predisposition to which kings throughout history have been prone).

SOCIAL CLASSES AND BLOODLINES

The Maya inscriptions inform us not only of dry historical fact—who was inaugurated when and who defeated whom—but also about the structure of the highest levels of Classic Maya society. These high levels were made up of two elite classes: *ahau* and *sahal* (or *cahal*). The ahau class stood at the pinnacle of society. Rulers were invariably ahaus, but the class included many others beyond those who took the throne. Membership in the class was inherited, and was held by both genders. One can easily imagine that many, perhaps most, ahaus were close relatives of the ruler, but too few parents are mentioned to trace relationships very far. At a lower level, sahals are nonetheless pictured in art and named in inscriptions, always in roles subsidiary to that of the ruler. Sometimes, as on Yaxchilan Lintel 8, they join the king in subduing enemies. Sometimes they serve as governors of secondary sites and have their own stelae, but their inscriptions are careful to specify that they owe allegiance to the ruler of the capital.

Ancestry was a matter of great pride and importance to Maya rulers. It is clear that the Maya envisioned ancestors as continuing an active role in support of the living. Deceased parents or more remote ancestors are sometimes portrayed in the sky above a ruler—even handing him the symbols of office. Living kings accordingly paid great attention to their chosen heirs. The battle and great ceremony portrayed in the wonderful murals at Bonampak are, in fact, all part of an heir-designation rite conducted on behalf of a baby prince. At Piedras Negras, several ceremonies were conducted for heirs apparent, attended by a variety of local and visiting nobles. Not surprisingly, epigraphers often speak of a Maya obsession with the purity of bloodlines; yet it may have been less an obsession than a very practical concern with political stability. Since rulers had multiple wives—hence, probably, many children—bitter power struggles over succession would not have been unlikely. Mechanisms such as heir-designation served to defuse problems in advance.

There are a few instances in which the inscriptions provide a peek at skeletons in the royal families' closets. The clearest example is the case of the ruler Shield Jaguar of Yaxchilan and his son Bird Jaguar, who eventually succeeded him on the throne. Shield Jaguar was a brilliant ruler who reigned for 61

The illustration on a vase, dated at A.D. 600-800, shows a drinking scene with a corpulent lord from Motul de San Jose leaning back to admire himself in a mirror held by a dwarf.

The murals at Bonampak, discovered in 1946, illustrate royal life around A.D. 790. In this scene, musicians and masked dancers participate in the rite of heir-designation being conducted for an infant prince.

years. During his lifetime, his inscriptions name two wives who engaged in rituals either with him or alone. After Shield Jaguar died, there was a period of 10 years in which there were no inscriptions at Yaxchilan and it is not clear who may have occupied the throne. But at the end of this interval, Bird Jaguar was inaugurated ruler with great ceremony. In many of his inscriptions, he proclaims himself the son of Shield Jaguar (a fact there is no reason to doubt), and also names and repeatedly celebrates his mother. Yet Bird Jaguar's mother was not among the wives mentioned by Shield Jaguar in his inscriptions. If she was an important woman—as Bird Jaguar claims—she seems not to have been very important to Shield Jaguar. Bird Jaguar claims that she performed important rites with Shield Jaguar, rites carried out on the same days as Shield Jaguar performed those rites with the wives he wrote about. "My mother," Bird Jaguar protests—perhaps too stridently—"was an important and honorable woman, worthy of being the mother of a king." Interestingly, Bird Jaguar was unusually active in commemorating the sahals who supported him: They are pictured joining him in ceremonies and in bat-

LEFT: The carved scene on a door lintel of Structure 23 at Yaxchilan shows the ruler, Shield Jaguar, holding a torch while his principal wife, Lady Xoc, pulls a length of thorn-lined rope through her pierced tongue in a bloodletting rite.

tle. The whole record suggests a bitter power struggle in which an energetic and ambitious man struggled his way onto the throne and then loudly proclaimed his right to be there. Whatever may have happened, Bird Jaguar's campaign worked; not only was he inaugurated in grand style, he went on to a career as illustrious as that of his father.

ROYAL MARRIAGE AND ROYAL VISITS

As the inscriptions provide glimpses of the intricacies of royal succession and the inevitable power struggles, they also suggest that Maya elite society was a vast web of relationships, alliances, friendships, and enmities. The uppermost level—that of the immediate families of rulers of major sites—was probably as interconnected as the great royal families of medieval Europe. One can imagine court gossip about princes and princesses, or tales of bitter feuds over real or imagined wrongs and insults.

Intermarriage between the great families was one mechanism by which the web of elite interconnections was maintained. This conclusion appears supported by the fact that some rulers' wives—who often appear in art and inscriptions—bear emblem glyphs indicating their origin in other sites; those not bearing emblem glyphs—the majority—are assumed to be local women. Although this is a fragile assumption, individuals without emblem glyphs have no known points of origin, and nothing by which to fit them into a familial network. In the relatively few cases where women bear emblem glyphs that differ from those of the sites at which they reside, one can usually recognize the political calculations involved. Sometimes, a smaller site or a site in a time of troubles will seek a marriage with a family at a high-prestige site. For example, after Copan lost its ruler, 18 Rabbit, in a battle with the much smaller Quirigua, Copan imported a woman from highly ranked Palenque to help restore prestige. And when the first ruler of Dos Pilas was busily maneuvering to establish his power base, he married a woman from neighboring Itzan and sent a Dos Pilas woman to marry the lord of small El Chorro. Both moves seem calculated to forge needed alliances and friendships among neighboring dynasties.

Occasionally, royal marriage seems to have backfired for a site seeking power. In the eighth century, the ruler of Arroyo de Piedra took as wife a woman from Dos Pilas. While the two sites were only about five miles apart, they were independent; Arroyo de Piedra was probably uneasy with Dos Pilas' growing strength, and eager to cement friendship. But when the son of the king and his Dos Pilas wife became ruler, he almost immediately proclaimed himself a vassal of the Dos Pilas lord; clearly his allegiance was to his mother's family—Arroyo de Piedra had lost its independence.

In the foregoing description of political marriages, women may sound like mere pawns in games of power chess. At times, this may well have been the case; but there are also clear instances of women who wielded great power in

This fine portrait of Ruler 6 of Piedras Negras was carved into a throne that was located in the west colonnade of Court One. Ruler 6 reigned from A.D. 781 to about 795.

Maya society. Although outright rulership seems usually to have been beyond the prerogatives of women, there are at least two exceptions at Palenque when women served as rulers, holding all the titles and symbols of office. Even more commonly, women emerge as powers behind the throne, getting more notice in inscriptions than their royal husbands, and seeming to be the real decision-makers. The site of Naranjo provides a well-documented example. Naranjo had been twice defeated by the site of Caracol in the mid-seventh century. After the second defeat, it was obliged to construct a hieroglyphic stairway telling of the Caracol victory; but then it carved no further inscriptions for 40 years. Intent upon a return to glory, Naranjo imported the daughter of the lord of Dos Pilas to marry a local lord. Lady Six Sky, as the daughter was called, was a forceful woman. It is she who is pictured on stelae

Lintel 2 of Piedras Negras commemorates the participation of a group of young peers from several neighboring sites at a ceremony for an heir-apparent of Piedras Negras. Such formal rites for a king-to-be helped to cement relationships between sites and to insure that the succession occurred without disruption.

and described in inscriptions. Her son, Smoking Squirrel, born five years after her arrival, was inaugurated king at the age of five (we don't know why), and the site of Naranjo embarked rapidly upon a series of important conquests. Of course, a five-year-old can hardly have been effective on the field of battle, and, indeed, it is Lady Six Sky who is pictured standing upon a prone captive. Even after Smoking Squirrel reached adulthood, most of his stelae continue to be paired with ones celebrating his mother.

Inter-site connections were also fostered through royal visits. In glyphic statements recently identified by glyph specialists Linda Schele, from the University of Texas, and Peter Mathews, University of Calgary, kings proudly list their visitors. Lintel 2 of Piedras Negras depicts a scene in which six small, and presumably young, individuals kneel before the king, while an adolescent boy stands behind him. All hold spears and wear warrior costumes. The figure behind the king is undoubtedly his son, who will one day rule; the other young men are identified by their glyphs as ahaus from Yaxchilan, Bonampak, and Lacan-ha, all sites within the same region as Piedras Negras. This would appear some sort of initiation rite, where the peers of the young Piedras Negras lord celebrate their friendship and ally the sites they will someday rule. Similarly, at Yaxchilan, a set of lintels recording the inauguration of kings boasts of important visitors, some from as far away as Tikal. It was probably through such state occasions that long-standing alliances between sites—some of which lasted for generations—were formed and maintained.

WARFARE

Of course, not all of Maya history was friendship and cooperation. Warfare was almost constant. A king's prestige demanded military achievement; the ceremonies of his passage through life demanded human sacrifice—the higher the victim's status, the greater the king's glory. So important were these victories that the capture of a major adversary became a part of the ruler's title, commemorating the event ever after. Most of the art portraying captives is formal, showing the king standing on or beside a prone, bound captive. At Yaxchilan, where much of the carving is on large lintels, more detail is provided. On a lintel in Temple 44, Shield Jaguar—already clad in a vest of quilted cotton armor, and holding a knife—is handed the remainder of his battle gear by his wife. On Lintel 8, his successor Bird Jaguar—wearing the same sort of armor as his father—subdues his rival, Jeweled Skull. Almost

Doorway lintels were used to record important events such as the inauguration of kings, battles, and the arrival of important visitors. Lintel 26 at Yaxchilan shows Shield Jaguar receiving battle gear from his wife on February 12, 724.

Near the bottom of Piedras Negras Stela 12, a group of prisoners from the site of Pomona fearfully await their destiny. Interestingly, the stela is carved in the style of Pomona rather than that of Piedras Negras, and it is possible that Pomona artists were captured and forced to record their own defeat at the victor's site.

OVERLEAF: The idea that the Maya were among the world's most gentle people has now been dispelled and it is clear that blood sacrifices were probably a near-daily routine in Maya ritual life.

invariably, the stone carvings provide insufficient space for full-scale battle scenes (in fact, we have no solid evidence of the actual way in which war was carried out). But in the murals of Bonampak, there is one true battle scene, a wild mêlée in which warriors defeat and carry off nearly naked enemies.

The most poignant scenes in Maya art are those of captured prisoners awaiting judgment—and, presumably, sacrifice. After the battle at Bonampak, prisoners are arrayed on a stairway, abject and bleeding, while their captor stands above them in judgment. In a wonderful stela from Piedras Negras, a group of prisoners from the site of Pomona seem to plead for mercy. Mercy, however, was not to be expected. The gods needed victims, as did—even more urgently—the king. His reputation had to be established at the beginning of his career, then periodically reinforced, so sacrifices were carried out relentlessly. Some prisoners were decapitated, others bound to scaffolds and shot with arrows; still others lived until their hearts—still beating—were ripped from their chests. But these were not necessarily the most agonizing deaths. Some victims were sacrificed repeatedly, being led to the altar for bloodletting, then returned to captivity where they were allowed to recover—until the next ceremony. One unfortunate ruler of Ucanal was captured by troops from the site of Naranjo. Time after time, the inscriptions of Naranjo report that he was a sacrificial offering—obviously of a non-lethal kind—until he finally disappears from the record after 18 years in captivity.

There is now vigorous debate about the principal objectives of Maya warfare, although everyone would agree that it accomplished a variety of goals.

Without question, it provided victims for sacrifice. It also served to enlarge the domains of sites as they expanded by means of conquest. Which of these motives predominated, however, is not a matter of agreement.

CEREMONIAL LIFE

In addition to their position as head of state and leading warrior, Maya rulers also played a central role in their cities' religious life. They presided over ceremonies and—through bloodletting rituals—even sacrificed themselves. After death they continued to serve as mediators from the afterlife, but were not, strictly speaking, divine. More precise, perhaps, is the view of Southern Methodist University archaeologist David Freidel that kings, both alive and dead, were a link between humans and the gods. The Maya saw the other world as having a series of portals—ranging from caves to temple doorways—where the two worlds could be bridged by a person with the correct spiritual keys. The king did this during his life. Among those with whom he could communicate were ancestors, especially those from whom he was directly descended. Then, when his earthly life had ended, he himself went to join this otherworldly line.

In a society that made such enormous investments in religious buildings and ritual, it is surprising that an institution of priesthood is almost totally invisible among the Classic Maya. No title for a religious office has ever been recognized in any of the glyphs. Religious scenes show the ruler or his wife as celebrants, and nowhere is there anyone else whose costume or activities would call

In this Late Classic painted vessel from Tikal, a subject (perhaps a priest) offers a baby jaguar to a ruler whose hand appears to the right.

to mind the title "priest." It is unthinkable, of course, that Maya society should not have included a large establishment of religious professionals: Somebody had to conduct ceremonies at which the king did not officiate. There must have been temple administrators and official keepers of the rites who were expert in ceremonial protocol. And given the Maya predilection for associating each day with symbols and gods—each portending good or evil—there must have been specialists in auguries for both elite and commoner to consult. But the corps of professionals carrying out these offices is nonexistent in Maya art and records. A plausible explanation for this invisibility is control on the part of the ruler. In many early civilizations, the temple establishment became powerful enough to threaten the authority of the king; Maya rulers may well have recognized this danger and, prudently, limited priestly authority.

THE REMAINDER OF MAYA SOCIETY

The portrait of the Maya elite as reconstructed from inscriptions remains very limited. We know that rulers had multiple wives and that royal families must have been large. All of the family members must have had some claim to status and possessions, but the inscriptions almost never note any royal children who did not become rulers. What happened to all the second sons whose names we never see? Did they receive estates in outlying territory? Are the smaller sites within a few miles of great centers the hearts of such estates? Or was the church a station for the not-mighty-enough? Recently discovered inscriptions from Copan give us a hint, for a man who is a half-brother of the ruler seems to be in charge of a small group a mile or so from the site center. There is hope that more archaeological work at outlying elite groups—which have been very little investigated—may eventually enlarge this picture.

All of the nobility, whether noted in inscriptions or not, comprised only two to five percent of the population. Among the remainder of the populace, there must have been highly skilled professionals—architects or master craftsmen such as jade-workers or painters of pottery—with a status akin to middle-class. In addition, there would have been artisans who produced everyday goods such as stone tools or pottery for household use. But even these likely made up less than 10 percent of the population. The great majority were simple farmers, toiling for long hours in their fields, and obliged to donate food and labor to support the enterprises of the nobility. The inscriptions tell us nothing of common people. If tax records or censuses were kept, they were in bark-paper books that have long since disappeared. Our knowledge of commoners comes entirely from archaeological remains that suggest a peasantry that seems not to have been exploited or downtrodden. Our knowledge of these people comes entirely from archaeological investigation of the house platforms that fill Maya cities. Their pole-and-thatch houses were cool and comfortable, each house surrounded by open space for vegetable gardens and fruit trees. In even the smallest housemounds, a third of the pottery consisted of beautiful hand-painted dishes that had been made in specialized workshops.

So the decipherment of Maya hieroglyphic writing in recent years has resulted in a major revolution in our understanding of the Classic Maya. Maya elite life has come alive, and we now see real people, hungry for prestige and power, trying to forge links with elites elsewhere. We see the calculation involved in power politics; we see war and bloodletting. Gone are the gentle priest leaders, replaced by entirely human kings. Haughty, they are sometimes power-mad; sometimes—as we will see in the next chapter—successful; and sometimes, foolish and devastated. They can no longer fulfill our romantic visions of what humans ought to be, but they are very much like what humans actually are.

The limestone near the site of Dos Pilas is honeycombed with caves that were used by the Maya for ceremonies. In this one, called Cave of Blood, dozens of polychrome vessels broken during the rituals litter the surface.

THE HISTORY OF THE CLASSIC MAYA

This is a marvelous time to be a Mayanist. For those of us not involved directly in the work of translating inscriptions, it has been like discovering, in a back room of some library, a dusty old book containing the whole, previously unknown history of the Classic Maya. We have worked for years with such archaeological evidence as the size of sites and the sequences of ceramics and structures. We have unearthed elite burials to find wonderful contents—but have had no choice but to describe the skeletal

Altar Q at Copan bears witness to the Maya concern with lineage. The altar commemorates the accession of Yax Pac, seen here receiving the baton of leadership from the founder of Copan's line, but it also portrays the 14 other kings who ruled before Yax Pac, each sitting cross-legged on his glyphic name.

occupants with such sterile phrases as "adult male over 60 years of age." After such limitations, the impact of actual written history is remarkable. Now we know which great temples were built during which kings' bursts of expansion; we can even explain periods during which no inscriptions were made. Some burial sites identify their occupants, so that they are no longer nameless skeletons, but the remains of Stormy Sky or Animal Skull. And now we have both the major outline and fascinating details of Classic Maya history.

Maya rulers were preoccupied with bloodlines, the legitimacy of their ancestry, and their rights to the throne. Kingship was traced to the site's named founder, usually from the fourth or fifth centuries. Kings were counted from the founder by means of what are called *hel* numbers (named for the untranslated hel glyph that accompanies the number). Curiously, even at sites where bloodlines were broken, an effort seems to have been made to preserve the notion of an unbroken line of kings: Even when descent was not direct, the hel count continued uninterrupted. Double Bird of Tikal, for example, called himself 21st hel of Tikal, while his successor, Animal Skull, was the 22nd hel—yet the two men do not seem to have been related.

The concept of a line of kings leading back to a founder is brilliantly depicted on Altar Q at Copan—a square altar carved in A.D. 763 to commemorate the accession of Yax Pac, the 16th ruler of the site. On the front of the altar, Yax Pac sits facing Yax Kuk Mo', the fifth-century founder of the Copan line, who passes to him the baton of office; meanwhile, the remaining 14 rulers, each seated upon his own name glyph, form a line leading to Yax Pac. As if to underline the point, a crypt near the altar houses the bodies of 15 jaguars, one for each of the rulers preceding Yax Pac. And, making an even more grandiose

This marvelous effigy of the Old God was found in Burial 10 at Tikal. The Old God was worshipped throughout the Maya area; he lived below the earth and represented the sun in the Underworld.

statement, the giant hieroglyphic stairway at Copan gives a long history naming the full list of rulers and praising their individual accomplishments. Only a few sites, however, give such complete dynastic lists. We still are faced with gaps and uncertainties in Maya history.

THE EARLY CLASSIC AND THE NORTHEAST PETEN

The description of Early Classic history must start with the northeast section of the Peten, the northernmost department in Guatemala. Much of it still forested and virtually unreachable, the area is crammed with giant early sites. Tikal, Uaxactun and Rio Azul have all been investigated by multi-year archaeological projects, but many other major sites are so remote that they remain unexamined.

The custom of erecting stelae to recount Maya history began in the northeast Peten. The earliest stela still located within its own site is the fragmentary Stela 29 at Tikal (unceremoniously dumped by the Maya in a rubbish heap, it was found by Tikal Project workers in 1959). The front of the stela pictures a ruler; but on the back, nothing is preserved but the date: A.D. 292. The earliest Tikal ruler for whom we have both an inauguration date and a name is a man called Moon Zero Bird, inaugurated in 320. We know about him from a jade plaque excavated by workmen digging a canal near Puerto Barrios in 1864, far from Tikal in the southeast corner of the lowlands. The Leiden Plaque—so called for its current museum home in the Netherlands—notes the accession of Moon Zero Bird and depicts him standing before a prone prisoner. How the plaque came to be laid in a small mound so far from its home remains a mystery. We are on somewhat firmer ground with the ruler Jaguar Paw. We know that he was the ninth hel of Tikal, that he was ruling in 376, and that his palace was Structure 5D-46 in the Central Acropolis: There, the inscription on a vessel found in a dedicatory cache reads "his house, Jaguar Paw, Ruler of Tikal, 9th Ruler."

The story of the next two rulers of Tikal provides a splendid example of the enrichment of knowledge derived from the decipherment of Maya hieroglyphic writing. The example returns us to the North Acropolis, the giant platform surmounted by 11 temples on the north side of the Great Plaza. In excavating the North Acropolis, the Tikal Project discovered two important Early Classic tombs: Burials 10 and 48. The tomb for burial 10 had been created by cutting through the front of a temple into bedrock beneath. Inside, the principal body—an adult male—was surrounded by nine additional skeletons (doubtlessly they were sacrificial victims). The tomb was stocked with an astonishing array of riches, including the ceramic effigy of an old god. Seated upon a stool with legs shaped like human femurs, the figure holds in his hands the offering of a human head. Other vessels, decorated with polychrome scenes painted on stucco, featured the Mexican rain god Tlaloc. In fact, both the old god and the painted scenes were less reminiscent of the lowland Maya than of

THE DYNASTY OF COPAN

Altar Q of Copan provides striking testimony to the Maya concept of a line of kings stretching back to a founder. The altar was the accession monument of Yax Pac, the 16th ruler of the Copan line. On the front of the altar Yax Pac (16) faces Yax Kuk Mo' (1), the early 5th-century founder of the Copan line. Between them are arrayed, four to an altar side, all the other kings of Copan, each seated upon his name glyph.

1. Yax Kuk Mo'
2. Unknown
3. Mat Head
4. Cu Ix
5. Unknown
6. Unknown
7. Waterlily Jaguar
8. Unknown
9. Unknown
10. Moon Jaguar
11. Butz' Chan
12. Smoke Jaguar
13. 18 Rabbit
14. Smoke Monkey
15. Smoke Shell
16. Yax Pac

1

2

4

5

7

8

9

10

12

13

14

15

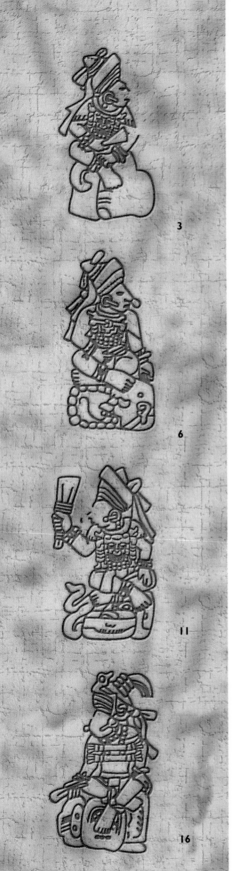

the great city of Teotihuacan, 800 miles (1287 kilometers) away in the Basin of Mexico. The people of Teotihuacan were ethnically and culturally very different from the Maya, although it is impossible to determine which of the many Mexican languages they may have spoken.

Meanwhile, Burial 48 occupied the most prestigious location in Tikal. The tomb shaft was cut through earlier construction into bedrock underneath the exact center of the stairs that led from the Great Plaza up to the North Acropolis. The primary individual in Burial 48 was accompanied by two sacrificial victims and, again, a variety of objects bearing Teotihuacan-inspired designs. Most importantly—we will soon see why—a Maya calendar date of A.D. 457 was painted on the wall of the tomb.

At some time, probably starting soon after the tombs were created, they were covered by a succession of newer and larger temples. One such construction, replacing the temple that then stood over Burial 48, occurred at about 650. When the old temple was about to be covered, a stela that was already more than two centuries old and partly broken—Stela 31—was hauled into its inner room. The stela was re-erected there, a great ceremonial fire was built around it, and incense burners used in the ceremony were smashed on the floor; then the room was filled with rubble so that construction could proceed. On the front of the stela appears a Maya figure clad in the elaborate costume of a king. On the sides are two men wearing the costume of Teotihuacan and carrying spearthrowers (typically Mexican weapons). Cloths hanging over their arms bear the face of Tlaloc. The entire back of the stela was devoted to a beautifully preserved inscription indicating that the stela had been carved in 445, 12 years before the date painted on the wall of Burial 48. The connection with Teotihuacan, and the identities of the important men in Burials 10 and 48, would remain mysteries until Stela 31 could be deciphered. Then the events became a part of history.

The inscription tells us that the stela was erected by Stormy Sky, a great Early Classic ruler, and the text relates a complicated history describing the king and his immediate predecessors in the Tikal royal line. Stormy Sky still reigned when Stela 31 was carved in 445, and was almost surely the man in Burial 48 because his successor ascended to the throne shortly after the burial date of 457. According to the stela's inscription, Stormy Sky's father had been a ruler called Curl Nose, whose name glyph appears on a jade figure in Burial 10; therefore, Curl Nose was the individual in Burial 10. The two tombs, then, contained the remains of two major fifth-century rulers, whose names had now been revealed.

The significance of the Teotihuacan connection is still debated, but it centers around a critical date in Tikal's Early Classic history. Even before the inscriptions could be read, it was clear that the Maya date 8.17.1.4.12 (January 16, A.D. 378) was very important for Tikal and its neighbor Uaxactun—the date is mentioned on stelae at both sites. The decipherment of Stela 31 revealed

The wonderfully preserved Stela 31 from Tikal shows on its front Stormy Sky who ruled from A.D. 426 to 457. Before the ruler's face dangles the chain-like end of a headdress that he holds aloft, while in the crook of his arm is the head of a god. On the back of a stela is a long hieroglyphic text that is the best description of the Early Classic history of Tikal.

On each side of Stela 31 is a warrior dressed in the costume of Teotihuacan and holding a spearthrower—a typical Mexican weapon—in his hand. Linda Schele believes that these warrior figures are, in fact, portraits of Stormy Sky's deceased father, Curl Nose. In any case, the figures are evidence of the strong ties between Tikal and Teotihuacan.

that on that date, Tikal defeated Uaxactun in a war. Also, by reading between the inscription lines, we discover a break in the royal bloodline at about that point. Just before the battle, Tikal was ruled by Jaguar Paw, the ninth ruler of the site; less than two years later, Curl Nose was inaugurated as the tenth ruler. Yet, according to Stela 31, Curl Nose's father was not Jaguar Paw, but a man with the very Mexican name of Spearthrower Owl (not only is the spearthrower a typically Mexican weapon, the owl is also common in Mexican symbolism). The accounts of the conquest of Uaxactun—on several stelae, including Stela 31—indicate that the leader of Tikal's forces was Smoking Frog, who is called the brother of Spearthrower Owl. There are many interpretations of these facts. My own is that there was a change in the ruling family at Tikal after the death of Jaguar Paw; and that Curl Nose, whose father and uncle were tied in some way with Teotihuacan and with the defeat of Uaxactun, came to the throne.

More information on this Mexican connection came to light when the Guatemalan National Tikal Project discovered a group of structures, somewhat separated from the site center, that seem to have been occupied by people from Teotihuacan. Both the architecture of the group and fragmentary murals found on a wall mirror the style of the Mexican city. Among the items found in excavations in the group was a "Ball Court Marker," a carved stone with a cylindrical shaft surmounted by a sphere and disk. Known previously from examples found in a ball court at Teotihuacan and sites on the gulf coast of Mexico, but never before encountered in the Maya lowlands. A Maya inscription is carved on the Ball Court Marker, mentioning the date of the war with Uaxactun, and naming both Spearthrower Owl and Smoking Frog. The carving ties the two men to the place where Teotihuacanos probably lived in Tikal.

At the height of Teotihuacan's power in the fourth through sixth centuries, colonies of the city's residents were quite common in foreign sites throughout Mesoamerica. Another example is Kaminaljuyu, a major Maya site on the outskirts of Guatemala City, in the highlands. There, the entire center of the site was rebuilt with structures of Teotihuacan style, and burials included goods similar to those found at Tikal. It is likely that the Teotihuacanos in foreign sites were merchants, because Teotihuacan was an immense manufacturing and trade center. But, in addition, merchants in ancient Mesoamerica were armed and served as paramilitary forces; they might well have aided Tikal in a war with Uaxactun or interfered in a local struggle over succession to the throne. Furthermore, the Teotihuacanos probably intermarried with local Maya, their prestige permitting entry into elite families. It is impossible to specify the background of men like Spearthrower Owl, Smoking Frog, and Curl Nose. They might have been from Teotihuacan itself or from the powerful colony at Kaminaljuyu; or they may have been the progeny of intermarriages between Teotihuacanos and local Tikal noblewomen, with significant claim to noble— perhaps even royal—Maya ancestry. Although opinions vary about this case, I

This Ball Court Marker found at Tikal combines a typically Mexican shape with a Maya inscription. The inscription mentions the date of the war with Uaxactun and names both Spearthrower Owl and Smoking Frog, emphasizing the ties that both men had with Teotihuacan.

believe that Curl Nose had at least some Teotihuacan ancestry in his background, and that he broke the descent line of Jaguar Paw when he became ruler of Tikal.

Whatever may have disrupted the Tikal royal line, the defeat of Uaxactun led to a period of great success for Tikal in the late fourth and early fifth centuries. A burst of new construction took place under the auspices of Curl Nose and Stormy Sky. The Great Plaza and other major plazas were re-paved; buildings were constructed to close the east and west ends of the Great Plaza, and the site received its first ball court. After the rule of Stormy Sky, the next several rulers erected stelae that give little information beyond dates and portraits. Almost all that can be said about the late fifth century is that Tikal seems to have continued confidently with its building programs.

There is even less—far less—to be said about Early Classic history at other sites. Between 292 and 435, all known examples of historical inscriptions occurred at locations within 30 miles (48 kilometers) of Tikal, except for single stelae at Rio Azul and at one site in Belize, both about 60 miles (97 kilometers) away. Needless to say, this does not mean that sites in other parts of the lowlands were unoccupied or that they did not have rulers; they simply did not write about them on stone. In the century between 435 and 534, the custom of erecting carved monuments spread rapidly through the lowlands. Tikal and other sites in the northeast Peten may well have helped foster this practice—early monuments show similarities in the styles of art and writing—but the dynasties themselves were probably of local origin.

THE MONUMENT HIATUS

Between 534 and 593, fewer carved monuments were erected in the central part of the lowlands—the area that had been the heart of the Early Classic historical records. This hiatus, as it is called, may have been a period of political turmoil, but without inscriptions it is difficult to say. Some sites at the edges of the lowlands were quite unaffected, however. Both Caracol—an exceedingly powerful site in Belize—and Copan, to the southeast, produced an uninterrupted set of monuments during the hiatus.

Tikal, on the other hand, had an unusually long period nearly devoid of stelae. Two stelae were erected there in 527; 30 years later, about 557, a single stela was erected, the last until the silence was broken with a stela in 692—initiating the period of Late Classic history at the site. The existing inscriptions hint at what may have happened. About the year 500, Jaguar Paw Skull—the self-proclaimed 14th ruler of Tikal—was on the throne. He may still have held it when the two stelae were erected in 527, but the stela set up in 557 records the inauguration of a leader named Double Bird in 537—as the 21st ruler. Thus, in what cannot have been more than one or two decades, seven kings had passed through the throne, leaving almost no record. Dynastic chaos seems a likely explanation. Whatever the problem, Double Bird solved it well enough to reign for more than 25 years, but after his single stela, Tikal lapsed into its long period of silence.

The mystery has been solved, at least partially, by the recent discoveries at Caracol made by archaeologists Arlen and Diane Chase, of the University of Central Florida. Caracol, enormously influential—and perhaps larger than Tikal in size and population—claims in a newly discovered inscription that it defeated Tikal twice: in 556 and 562. The second defeat coincides with the point at which Double Bird's record ceases, and at which a number of earlier monuments at Tikal were deliberately defaced and broken. In addition, we now know something about the 22nd ruler—Animal Skull—who followed Double Bird onto the Tikal throne. Although Animal Skull left no carved stone monuments, his very rich burial contains a plate with an inscription; Animal Skull names himself 22nd hel and gives his father's name. But his father—who bears no emblem glyph to show his origin—was not Double Bird. It seems likely, then, that Animal Skull was a ruler imposed upon Tikal after its defeat, although he could have been either from Caracol or a local Tikal lord from some lineage that Caracol favored.

THE LATE CLASSIC

During the Late Classic, beginning about 600, the political record of sites becomes much more clear. The next 200 years were to be a golden epoch for

Although the site of Caracol in Belize has long been known, its size and political importance were not recognized until recently. This photo shows Structure A-3 in one of the site's major groups after it had been cleared and stabilized.

RIGHT: Tatiana Proskouriakoff's watercolor shows the hieroglyphic stairway in Copan leading to a temple above the ball court. The stairway, constructed shortly after the Copan ruler 18 Rabbit was captured and sacrificed at Quirigua, is a reassertion of Copan's glory. The text—the longest in Maya Classic carving—names all the rulers of Copan and tells of their accomplishments. The figures in the center of the stairs are the most important kings clad in their warrior costumes.

Strangely shaped stone silhouettes of astounding craftsmanship, such as this one found on the floor of an early temple at Copan, are called "eccentrics." It is assumed that their significance was ceremonial because no practical use for them can be imagined.

the Maya of the southern lowlands. Population and construction boomed, and inscriptions are both more abundant and more informative. This was a time of famous rulers, great men all (according to their own testimony). But it was also a time buffeted by the ebb and flow of historical chance: Sites blossomed for a while, then fell on hard times, only to rise again to power. The great rulers jockeyed for position while armies swept back and forth across the lowlands.

COPAN IN THE LATE CLASSIC

Since 1975, a series of archaeological projects have made Copan among the best known of all Maya Late Classic sites. Researchers have aimed to integrate archaeological data (including fascinating information from a vast tunneling exploration of the early levels below the acropolis) with the decipherment of the site's abundant and well-preserved inscriptions. In addition, excavations in a neighboring group of non-royal but nonetheless elite residences provide a glimpse into the life of nobles who were not directly part of the royal circle.

For centuries, Copan was a major site and, probably—given its location at the far southeastern edge of the lowlands—a trade center where the Maya came in contact with non-Maya people from elsewhere in Central America. Justly famous for its deeply carved stelae with their splendid glyphs (they are works of art as well as a written text), the site includes a huge plaza and the largest ball court in the Classic period lowlands. A hieroglyphic stairway leading to a temple above the ball court boasts the longest single inscription ever discovered in Maya explorations. Then, above the great plaza rises an acropolis, a giant raised area where wonderful small courtyards are ringed by stately buildings decorated with elaborate carvings.

The first of the great Late Classic rulers of Copan was a man named Smoke Jaguar. Long-lived, Smoke Jaguar came to the throne in 628 and ruled until 695. Although most of his buildings are now buried under subsequent construction, Smoke Jaguar left 11 stelae and three altars to celebrate his reign. A number of the stelae were placed in small sites at the edges of the Copan Valley, perhaps to make his presence visible to the locals in outlying areas; his territory apparently extended at least to the site of Quirigua, 45 miles (72 kilometers) away in the Motagua River Valley, where a recently deciphered inscription on an altar names Smoke Jaguar.

Smoke Jaguar was succeeded by 18 Rabbit, who seemed bent upon surpassing his predecessor's grandeur. Most of the impressive visual images at Copan are the creations of 18 Rabbit. His are the almost-in-the-round stelae that fill the great plaza. His is the marvelous Structure 10L-22, set high in the acropolis and adorned with what may be the best architectural sculpture at the site. It was 18 Rabbit who constructed the final version of the ball court. Without explaining why, 18 Rabbit lists four great lowland sites on Stela A: Copan, Palenque, Tikal, and Site Q—a site of debatable location, known only through

looted material. It is unknown whether this inscription is intended to suggest the mighty friends and allies of Copan, or whether 18 Rabbit may even have been boasting (quite without basis in fact) that these sites were under the control of Copan. In any case, neither his accomplishments nor his pride kept 18 Rabbit (the unlucky 13th ruler of Copan) from coming to a bad end: On May 3, 738, he was captured and promptly sacrificed by Cauac Sky of Quirigua.

To say nothing of the physical damage Copan may have suffered from this military disaster, the psychological blow must have been devastating. Quirigua was a tiny site that throughout most of its history was probably a provincial center under Copan's control. Before his victory, Cauac Sky was a nobody, and little is known about him. He was inaugurated "in the land of 18 Rabbit," a phrase which demonstrates his secondary status in relation to the Copan monarch. That the great king of Copan had been captured by such an upstart must have rocked the Maya lowlands. It is not clear how it happened. Tiny Quirigua would not likely have had an army capable of defeating the Copan warriors; one is more apt to think of a sudden raid, or perhaps even treachery within Copan. In the aftermath, Copan hastened to salve its wounds. After the brief reign of a 14th ruler, it brought in a Palenque woman to marry the 15th king and add renewed prestige. Copan also soon began the work of erecting its illustrious hieroglyphic stairway, the reconstruction and interpretation of which has been under way since 1986 in a project headed by William and Barbara Fash from Northern Illinois University. It is becoming clear that the hieroglyphic stairway is a reassertion of the greatness of Copan. The text passes over the sacrifice of 18 Rabbit in a single, swift phrase, and

Some of the risers on the Hieroglyphic Stairway at Copan show prone figures. Unlike hieroglyphic stairways at other sites, where such figures are bound with ropes and represent prisoners, those at Copan are unbound and may be ancestral figures.

Stela C in Copan, portraying the powerful ruler 18 Rabbit, was the first of many stelae to be erected by him in the Great Plaza. He was responsible for most of the visual images at Copan. This one still shows clear traces of the red paint that originally decorated it.

focuses instead upon the exploits of such important rulers as Smoke Jaguar.

By the time of the next ruler—Yax Pac, inaugurated in 763—Copan was back in its glory. Yax Pac undertook an ambitious building program in the acropolis, dedicated a number of stelae, and gave Copan another brief moment in the sun. But the shadow of the Classic Maya collapse was beginning to creep across the lowlands, and Yax Pac's success was soon to fade into the mist.

PALENQUE AND THE TOMB OF PACAL

As Copan marks the far southeastern border of lowland Maya civilization, Palenque plays a similar role to the northwest. Palenque nestles against the verdant mountains of Chiapas, a backdrop kept forever green by the region's nearly unceasing rains. The impact of the site and its spectacular setting are

LEFT: Temple of the Inscriptions, Palenque, rests on a 65-foot-high (19.8 meters) stepped pyramid approached by an impressive frontal stairway. It contains the funerary crypt of the mightiest of Palenque's rulers, Lord Pacal, who died in A.D. 683.

unforgettable. Although faithful to the basic architectural principles of the lowlands, Palenque expresses them in its own fashion. The roofs above doorways are sloping rather than vertical, and the decorative roofcombs use a lace-like openwork whose effect is lighter than the solid masses of the Peten. Palenque introduced its own twist into artistic canons as well. There are no stelae at the site. Instead, carving is done on wall panels in an unmistakable low-relief style whose expressiveness and delicacy have few parallels.

Palenque is probably best known for being the site of the most romantic of all Maya tombs. The adventure of the tomb's discovery began in 1949, when Alberto Ruz Lhuillier—the Mexican archaeologist in charge of the excavations—was cleaning the floor inside the Temple of the Inscriptions, the largest structure at the site. Part of the flooring consisted of a great slab with a double row of holes drilled along one edge. Thinking that the perforations must mean something, Ruz penetrated the floor and discovered a set of steps; the holes, in fact, had been drilled so that ropes could be used to lift the slab and expose the stairway. Nowhere else at a Maya site has there been found a secret entrance to a stairway leading into the depths of a pyramid. However, the Maya had completely filled the entire passage with a nearly impenetrable mixture of rock and soil. Ruz had no choice but to do whatever it took to discover where the stairway led.

Bit by painstaking bit, workers began removing the fill in the narrow space, which continually sweated moisture. At the end of the 1949 season, Ruz reported that the stairway had been cleared to a depth of 25 feet (8 meters), revealing nothing of greater interest than 21 carefully fashioned steps; little did he realize that the project would last three more seasons before the bottom was reached. In the next season—now 50 feet (15 meters) below the temple floor—a landing and alcove gave momentary hope that the prize was at hand; but the stairway simply changed direction and continued downward. Thirteen steps and 12 feet (4 meters) below the landing, something, at last, appeared. A tiny stone chamber held a few vessels, some carved jades, and a teardrop-shaped pearl—a nice cache, but hardly sufficient reward for the four long seasons of work. But then, immediately below the cache box, the excavators encountered a jumble of human bones. In all, six bodies had been stuffed into a narrow space, then immediately covered with mortar as the stairway was being filled. The bodies were, of course, a sign that the quest was nearing its end. Immediately below them, Ruz encountered a huge, triangular slab carefully fitted to what seemed to be a doorway. When the slab was removed, the scene that appeared is best described in Ruz' own words:

> After having had to dismantle, stone by stone, hundreds of cubic meters of the fill that obstructed the stairs, the first impression the crypt had upon me was the surprise of finding a hollow space, a kind of enormous cave, that through the solidity and geometric regularity of its sides, seemed carved in the rock, or better in the ice, because of the calcareous formations produced

by the trickling of the water through the nucleus of the pyramid. Soon I realized that great reliefs adorned the walls and that a colossal carved altar filled the major part of the crypt. In passing the threshold, I had the strange sensation of penetrating time, into a time that had stopped a thousand years before. The feeling was heightened by the fact that the crypt had remained exactly as it was then, except for the stalactites and stalagmites added over the centuries, and that nothing had moved in it, nor had anyone entered, and that what our eyes were the first to see was the same thing seen by the last Maya priest as he left the chamber.

In his description, Ruz refers to the great sculptured stone as an altar, because the excavators had not at that time dared to try moving the heavy piece. It later proved to be the outer lid of a large stone sarcophagus, neatly fitted with a carefully worked inner lid, and containing the skeleton of a man bedecked with a king's treasury of jade jewelry. The sculptured scene on the cover has since become one of the most familiar masterpieces of Maya art, despite the fact that it lies forever entrapped in the tomb where it was found, an entire temple blocking its removal. The sculpture depicts the tomb's occupant falling backward into the underworld—just as, in the Maya view, the setting sun falls each night into the realm of the gods of death, only to be reborn the following morning.

We now know that the person in this tomb was Pacal the Great, who ruled Palenque from 615 to 683. Pacal prepared the Temple of the Inscriptions as his funerary temple, first setting in place the great block from which the sarcophagus was to be carved, then building the temple overtop it. On the sides of the sarcophagus were carved the pictures of Pacal's ancestors, along with a text listing their dates of death. In the room of the temple above, a lengthy inscription provides a complicated genealogical message: Pacal's forebears are listed once again, and his mother is likened to "Lady Beastie"—the female progenitor of the human race according to Maya mythology. Linda Schele makes a strong case that Pacal's seeming obsession with genealogy was due to the fact that he had inherited the throne from his mother, a happenstance that—Schele believes—violated the rules of descent through the male line. Consequently, Pacal's hieroglyphic gyrations attempt to demonstrate that in his case such inheritance through the female line was god-like, rather than irregular.

Upon the sealing of Pacal's tomb, his son Chan Bahlum succeeded him and constructed the marvelous three-temple Group of the Cross. Since Chan Bahlum was of the same "incorrect" lineage as Pacal, he went to even greater extremes than his father to trace his genealogy back to the gods; the scenes and inscriptions within his temples delve into times before the creation of the present universe in order to justify his right to rule. After the death of Chan Bahlum in 702, three additional rulers led the site before Palenque faded into obscurity toward the end of the eighth century.

The lid of Pacal's sarcophagus shows the dead king atop the setting sun as he falls into the gaping jaws of the Earth Monster. From his body grows the World Tree topped by a celestial bird.

EMPIRE AT DOS PILAS

The dream of empire appealed to the vanity of Late Classic rulers. With rising populations and escalating competition between sites, an intensification of warfare was inevitable. Vanquishing rivals and taking their land and riches provided a boost to the victors' economies as well as balm to their royal egos. The best-established example of empire-building, as related by epigraphers Stephen Houston and Peter Mathews, occurred in the zone of sites bordering the Pasión River toward the southern edge of the lowlands. There, the skillful and cunning Flint Sky began a meteoric career in 645, when he was inaugurated ruler of Dos Pilas—a site previously too insignificant to have had inscriptions. Flint Sky came to Dos Pilas from elsewhere, possibly from Tikal (some of the elements of his name glyphs are similar to those used by Tikal royalty, and throughout its history, Dos Pilas used the same emblem glyph as Tikal). Once installed at Dos Pilas, the fledgling ruler moved forcefully. He waged a series of wars and careful-

The last remains of Dos Pilas' Ruler 2 are painstakingly uncovered by Arthur Demarest of Vanderbilt University. The tomb also yielded pottery, jade jewelry, and bloodletting instruments.

ly cultivated allies by well-contrived marriages. He took as wife a woman from Itzan on the other side of the Pasión River, and sent a woman of his line to marry into the dynasty of the site called El Chorro. Later in his career, his daughter, Lady Six Sky, was sent to Naranjo to rejuvenate the failed dynasty there.

Flint Sky developed an important relationship with Jaguar-Paw Jaguar, who would eventually become ruler of Site Q—the mysterious looted site that may lie either in some still-undiscovered location in northern Guatemala, or that may be the giant site of Calakmul, just north of the border with Mexico. The two men participated in ceremonies together before Jaguar-Paw Jaguar was inaugurated, and Flint Sky went to Site Q to witness his inauguration in 686. A looted pot that shows Jaguar-Paw Jaguar kneeling in obeisance before an unnamed Dos Pilas ruler has sparked speculation that Flint Sky may even have controlled Site Q. The crowning glory of Flint Sky's career, however, remained unknown until 1991, when researchers read a newly discovered hieroglyphic stairway at Dos Pilas. The stairway relates that in 679 Dos Pilas captured and sacrificed Shield Skull, then ruler of Tikal. From this unexpected information one must surmise that if Flint Sky had originally come from Tikal, he must have been a member of some unsuccessful faction; perhaps he was even an exile who bore his home site no good will.

The good fortunes of Dos Pilas continued under Ruler 2, who took over the nearby site of Arroyo de Piedra, and Ruler 3, who conquered Seibal, some 20 miles (32 kilometers) away in a key location on the Pasión River. During Ruler 3's time, the site of Aguateca was made a joint capital, and stelae began to be erected there as well as at Dos Pilas. Aguateca occupies a formidable position on cliffs above the Río Petexbatun, a tributary of the Pasión; it would later serve as a fortress in the final defense of the kingdom. The start of Ruler 4's reign was also successful. He is repeatedly mentioned at Seibal, which was still obviously under Dos Pilas' control, and he may have captured a lord of Cancuen, far upriver along the Pasión. At its height in the early days of Ruler 4, the empire carved out by the Dos Pilas monarchs covered an area 50 miles (80 kilometers) north-south and 30 miles (48 kilometers) east-west. But its end was near.

Archaeological evidence of desperation in the face of impending doom was discovered recently by the Dos Pilas Project, under the direction of Arthur Demarest, of Vanderbilt University. Hastily built defensive walls sprawl across Dos Pilas. In what must have been a last ditch attempt to defend the site, stones were even torn from temples and palaces to bolster the fortifications. The attempt seems to have been in vain, for an inscription at the site of Tamarindito claims defeat of Ruler 4; the site of Dos Pilas was abandoned, although activity continued at Aguateca. Even with the new Ruler 5 stationed at Aguateca and a surrounding system of defensive walls, the empire rapidly disintegrated. Site after site broke away from the Dos Pilas domain and began to erect its own inscriptions once again. By about 800, Aguateca also was abandoned, and the Dos Pilas dynasty was no more.

THE RECOVERY OF TIKAL

Tikal, silent for more than a century since its defeat by Caracol—and suffering from the additional humiliation of having lost its ruler Shield Skull to Dos Pilas—began a resurgence with the inauguration of Ruler A (sometimes called Ah Cacao) in 682. Ruler A was the son of the hapless Shield Skull, and the grandson of Animal Skull—the ruler who may have been imposed by Caracol. Ten years after his accession, Ruler A resumed the long-neglected tradition of monuments by dedicating a stela and altar. Although the altar was in the style of Caracol, Ruler A seems shortly thereafter to have rejected Caracol ties and asserted his descent within a proper Tikal lineage. Reaching back in time, he invoked the image of the great Early Classic ruler, Stormy Sky. He began by rebuilding Temple 33 at the front of the North Acropolis, deep under which Stormy Sky was buried; but first, before undertaking the project, Ruler A carefully deposited Stormy Sky's Stela 31 in its final resting place under the new structure. This harkening back to Early Classic greatness also pervades the carved wooden lintels in Temple 1—the huge temple on the east side of the Great Plaza that was eventually to house Ruler A's tomb. A key event described on the lintels was the dedication of a temple, probably Temple 33. The date chosen for the dedication was exactly 13 katuns (260 years) after the date of the last ceremony recorded by Stormy Sky on Stela 31. In addition, lintel scenes depicting Ruler A as a warrior display the same symbols and accoutrements used by Stormy Sky centuries before.

Ruler A seemed to have vowed that he would return Tikal to the days of its former glory—it was a promise that he kept. His first military achievement was the capture in 695 (and subsequent sacrifice 158 days later) of Jaguar-Paw Jaguar, king of Site Q. This victory settled old scores between the sites: Site Q had been Caracol's ally when it defeated Tikal a century earlier. In addition, it

Tikal's Ruler A kept his promise to return the center to its former glory. Temple II is shown in the foreground with Temple III at left, and Temple IV at right.

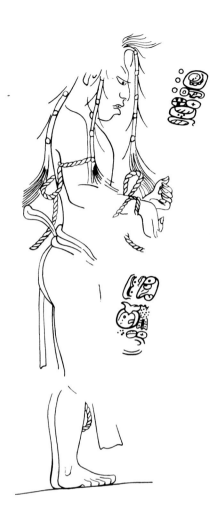

In one of the great masterpieces of Maya art, a captive lord from Site Q was immortalized on one of the carved bones found in the Tomb of Ruler A of Tikal.

had fought Tikal again in the time of Ruler A's father, Shield Skull, and had been an ally of the Dos Pilas regime that had sacrificed Shield Skull. After the defeat of Site Q, additional captives and military campaigns soon attested to Tikal's rebirth, and gigantic construction efforts added to Ruler A's prestige. The huge Temples 1 and 2 at the east and west edges of the Great Plaza called everyone's attention to Tikal (as they still do). Elsewhere at the site, building complexes were constructed one after the other. Early stelae lavished praise on Ruler A and Tikal, although in his later years, the ruler's stelae turned more toward departed wives and companions. As Christopher Jones, the University of Pennsylvania archaeologist who deals with the Tikal inscriptions, puts it: "death occupies his thoughts.... The old king of Tikal, at one time a young triumphant statesman and warrior, now burdened with the memories of the departed, could finally rest his tired body under the weight of the rich jades he wore for so many years of rule."

Ruler A led Tikal for more than 50 years until sometime around 734, when he went to join the ancestors. The discovery of his resting place was another triumph for the Tikal Project. The story begins in 1959, when a tunnel was punched through the bottom of the stairway of Temple 1 to determine whether earlier structures lay buried underneath. As the tunnel bored into the temple, flint and obsidian chips began to appear in the fill of the structure. This was a promising sign: For reasons unknown, the Maya habitually added such chips to the fill surrounding tombs. Deeper into the temple, the number of chips increased, raising hopes further; yet the early floor that underlay the temple was unbroken, with no sign that a burial had been intruded through it. Finally, 25 feet (8 meters) into the structure, the flint and obsidian ceased and the tunnel was abandoned, leaving gunnysacks full of stone chips sitting forlornly outside the Project's laboratory. Later, in 1962, the team began two lateral tunnels heading north from the original tunnel; the first tunnel found nothing, but when the second had penetrated 17 feet (5 meters), it reached the hoped-for cut through the early floor. Three feet beneath the cut was a great slab, its top darkened by a ceremonial fire. Intriguingly, when an investigator inserted a six-foot measuring tape into a crack between the slab and an adjoining stone, the tape disappeared into emptiness. Clearly, a chamber lay below.

Removal of the slab revealed a large vaulted chamber. At its bottom, a single skeleton was stretched out on its back in the center of a raised dais. Surrounding the skeleton was a spectacular collection of treasures. Pearls were scattered around its neck and chest, as were 114 spherical beads of jade, some as large as 2 inches (5 centimeters) in diameter. Twenty vessels were placed on the floor beside the dais, 10 of which were painted cylinders showing scenes of a king seated on a throne. Dozens of tiny jade pieces proved to be the remains of a cylinder completely covered in jade mosaic. At the south end of the tomb, the last thing to be uncovered was what at first had appeared to be a carefully arranged pile of not-too-unusual bone tools; but as the dust was brushed from them, delicate engravings came to life, the designs accented with a red pigment. Because many of the bones have pointed ends, they might be considered awls or needles in a domestic context, but it seems more likely, given their decoration, that they were ornamental or intended for some unknown ritual use. Whatever their function, the bones are, in fact, one of the most exquisite collections of Maya art ever discovered. Some bones contained only hieroglyphic inscriptions; others showed scenes. One scene portrayed a splendid standing captive looking mournfully down at his tied hands. Another was a beautifully drawn hand of an artist holding a paintbrush. Two scenes were of gods fishing from canoes. Another showed two gods paddling a large canoe whose passengers also included a lizard, a parrot, a singing dog, and, in their midst, a downcast-looking Maya, his hand to his forehead. This latter scene undoubtedly depicts the journey of the dead king into the underworld (although at first glance it resembles a group of revelers returning from a late-night party). Several of the inscriptions name Ruler A and celebrate his achievements. In death, Ruler A had been surrounded by a profusion of riches accumulated during his long career.

Ruler B, the son and successor of Ruler A, continued the program established by his father. It was he who built Temple 4, at 212 feet (65 meters) the tallest of all the Tikal temples. It seems likely that he is entombed within its enormous bulk, but no project to date has had the resources necessary to search for his tomb. The next successor, Ruler C, continued on the same path early in his career, building more great temples and erecting stelae that celebrated his military prowess. Later, though, inscriptions became less and less frequent; the fates of Ruler C and some possible successors are clouded by half-legible

This museum reconstruction of the burial of Tikal's Ruler A shows some of the offerings that accompanied the king. Especially noteworthy are the large jade beads near the waist.

Calakmul, shown here emerging from the forest, was a Preclassic city which grew to its full glory during the Classic period. Although a large number of carved stelae were located at the site, most of them are too badly eroded to be read. Judging from its great size, the site must have played a major role in Late Classic politics, and many archaeologists believe that it may have been the Site Q known largely from looted monuments.

inscriptions that do not make a sensible story. Tikal, too, was being engulfed by the spreading Classic collapse.

This chapter, of course, has only skimmed the surface of a long and complicated Maya history. We know far more about dynasties than can be discussed in the space available here, and there are major sites that have barely been mentioned. An overall picture, however, has begun to emerge about Maya Classic sites and politics. A relatively few Classic sites stand above the others—those with the biggest buildings, the largest number of inscriptions, the most spectacular art. Tikal, Copan, Palenque, Yaxchilan, Calakmul, Naranjo, Piedras Negras, Dos Pilas, and Caracol fall into this category for me, although other archaeologists might make some additions or deletions. But more important than such a list is the fact that all these sites—and others—were cities that endured for centuries, always centers of population and activity. One certainty about these cities is that the political careers of their rulers were checkered; periods of success, and mighty rulers who seemed to do no wrong, alternated with defeat and humiliation. Sometimes a site raged outward in warfare to build a domain at the expense of its neighbors, but in time the empire weakened and crumbled—often as rapidly as it had been created. Larger than, and different from, any of its individual units, the heart of Maya civilization depended not on the fate of a particular center at any given moment, but rather on a shared elite culture and a web of great families that overrode the vagaries of history.

During the Terminal Classic period, the population of Seibal actually increased; with the increase came a flurry of construction and the erection ing efforts was this temple with four stairways, each with a stela dated to A.D. 849. A fifth stela is located inside the building.

of new stelae. The centerpiece of the new build-

THE COLLAPSE OF THE CLASSIC

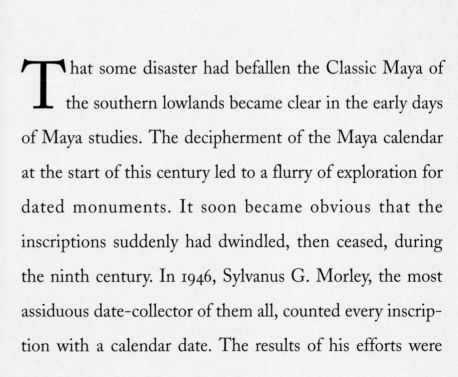

That some disaster had befallen the Classic Maya of the southern lowlands became clear in the early days of Maya studies. The decipherment of the Maya calendar at the start of this century led to a flurry of exploration for dated monuments. It soon became obvious that the inscriptions suddenly had dwindled, then ceased, during the ninth century. In 1946, Sylvanus G. Morley, the most assiduous date-collector of them all, counted every inscription with a calendar date. The results of his efforts were striking. At the end of the katun in 9.18.0.0.0 (A.D. 790), 19 different centers had erected dated monuments—the largest number ever to celebrate a katun end. In 810, 12 sites commemorated the next katun; but by 830, only three sites had retained the vigor to erect stelae. By 890, the very last date in the Maya Long Count was carved. Although more monuments have been discovered since 1946, the pattern remains the same: It is still evident that the erection of these dated monuments came to an abrupt end. In addition, the paucity of Postclassic structures in the southern lowlands makes it quite clear that elite construction probably ended at about the same time that inscriptions ceased.

The decipherment of inscriptions has now provided hints of the impending collapse. Not that the inscriptions say anything directly, of course. There are no lamentations, no prophets of doom decrying the state of affairs or predicting the end of the Maya world. On the surface, late texts sound as they always did. Kings continued dedicating buildings, capturing prisoners, and performing ceremonies that were quite as wonderful as ever. But by reading between the lines one can see signs of political fragmentation; the system was becoming ever more difficult to control.

The splendid data from Copan provide the most information. As we have seen, the ruler Yax Pac led a resurgence of the site after his inauguration in 763. But in the very inscriptions that announce Yax Pac's importance, William Fash sees hints of political difficulties. A carved bench in an elite residential group near the main center of Copan indicates that Yax Pac conducted a scattering rite—a glyph shows a hand dropping something, perhaps drops of blood—for the local noble in 780. Another bench in an even more sumptuous compound commemorates the dedication of a noble's house, and states that Yax Pac sent a ceramic offering to the celebration. In another inscription, a noble from an outlying site uses the Copan emblem glyph and claims a relationship with the ruler. Fash interprets these inscriptions as an indication that Yax Pac, probably under severe pressure from a worsening situation, had extended special privileges to his nobles in order to muster their continuing support. He had allowed them their own inscriptions and the use of the Copan emblem glyph, for example. By 800, the end seemed near for Yax Pac as he dedicated his last structure, a pathetic, tiny temple at the far end of the acropolis. William Fash describes this final temple:

> The most significant decoration on the building is on the two pairs of door jambs, whose sculpture is carved in shallow relief and not meant to be read from any great distance.... [T]he iconography is that of war and captive sacrifice, presented in a very blatant way. The diminutive size of the structure in comparison to previous Acropolis temples implies a lack of support for any grandiose building plans, even for what has been interpreted by some as Yax Pac's funerary temple.... [T]he emphasis on warrior iconography...was borne not of strength, but of weakness....

Next to the temple was Stela 11, probably dating to 820 and showing an almost grotesque Yax Pac, dead and in the underworld. The inscription makes reference to the fall of the house of Yax Pac, proclaiming that the long dynastic line of Copan had come to an end. But one final carving was attempted. Altar L, which dates to 822, shows a scene in which Yax Pac sits facing a new ruler, in the same way the founder faced Yax Pac on Altar Q. But, curiously, after the front and part of the back of the altar had been carved, work ceased; the unfinished altar is all that remains to tell of the end of rulership at Copan.

If the spread of inscriptions to a larger group of nobles indicates weakening authority at Copan, a similar pattern on a much wider scale suggests political disarray elsewhere in the lowlands. Toward the end of the Late Classic after 750, a number of small- to medium-size sites began to erect carved monuments (or to resume the practice after a long gap) in both the central area and the Pasion region. Uaxactun, for example, only 12 miles (19 kilometers) from Tikal and probably under the control of its larger neighbor for centuries, erected a stela in 751—its first in more than 200 years. Over the next 30 years, four additional sites in the central area began or resumed monument carving. These may represent cases in which rulers of larger sites extended privileges to governors of secondary sites, or they may mean that the governors had declared their independence. Either hypothesis spells a weakening of the central power.

By the mid-800s, the situation was almost chaotic. Near Tikal, three separate sites—Tikal itself, Jimbal, a minor site 7 miles (11 kilometers) to the north, and Ixlu, at the edge of Lake Peten Itza 15 miles (25 kilometers) south of Tikal—erected monuments. All used the Tikal emblem glyph, but named different rulers, each claiming, one imagines, to be the true heir to the Tikal line. A parallel can be found at a slightly earlier date in the Pasion region, when two or possibly three rulers at different sites simultaneously used the Dos Pilas emblem glyph; the fact is that the Dos Pilas kingdom was in the process of breaking up. As an ancient Assyrian scribe wondered in a similar time of troubles, "Who was king? Who was not king?"

These signs of disintegrating authority indicate an unraveling of the fabric of elite life. But what of the common people? As recently as 1966, Eric Thompson argued that the collapse occurred because the lower classes over-

Early in Yax Pac's career as ruler of Copan, he dedicated Temple 11, which included this carved bench that, like Altar Q, recorded his royal ancestors. Later, as the fortunes of Copan began to decline, lesser nobles were granted the prerogative of having their own carved benches.

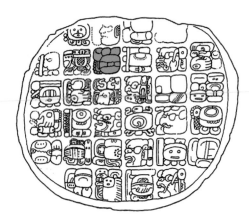

In the mid-ninth century, a ruler at the small site of Ixlu, south of Tikal, erected two stelae and the altar shown here. Although the ruler may have been either from a Tikal faction or an intruder from elsewhere, he used the Tikal emblem glyph (shaded in light brown) thus being one of several contemporary pretenders to the Tikal throne.

threw their priestly leaders, abandoned the ceremonial centers, and retired to live peacefully in the surrounding countryside. This suggestion was disproved by the same mapping and mound-counting projects that had demonstrated the high Late Classic population. The new data showed that by the time of the Terminal Classic (830-930), populations of both elites and commoners at most southern lowland sites had declined by at least two-thirds from the peaks of the eighth century; by the Postclassic (after 930), no more than a few scattered houses remained. A recent compilation of all available population data illustrates just how widespread the decline was. Sites were devastated and bereft of people in a vast area that stretched from the Usumacinta River on the west to the Belize/Guatemala border on the east, and from the Becan region in the north to the foothills of the Guatemalan mountains in the south. There were some exceptions. Remnant populations persisted along the chain of lakes in Guatemala's central Peten district; population loss was slow at Copan, the lower-class population seeming to have dwindled slowly for several centuries after the collapse of the elite. But these are very small territories and numbers of people compared to an area of nearly 30,000 square miles (80,000 square kilometers) where millions of people disappeared. The Classic Maya collapse can justifiably be termed a demographic disaster.

Where had the people gone? Had they become streams of refugees fleeing tragedy? Although some undoubtedly fled, far too many people were involved for any great percentage to have migrated. Neighboring areas were already occupied, and could hardly have absorbed a huge influx of new residents. Moreover, such a sudden surge of population would surely be detectable archaeologically, and no evidence for it exists. Instead, it seems clear that not only had inscriptions and elite construction died; the people had died with them. This statement, however, evokes inappropriately grisly images. One thinks instinctively of mass graves, of the tumbrels rolling daily through the streets of Europe at the time of the Black Death, or of the starving hordes of sub-Saharan Africa. In the Maya lowlands, however, the population decline was certainly spread over 50 years, perhaps a century—several generations for a population with a short life expectancy. Even at the best of times, infant mortality was likely to have been 40 percent, the result of nonexistent sanitation, parasites, infant diarrhea, and the everyday diseases of the moist tropics. If infant mortality increased 10 or 20 percent in stressful times—perhaps accompanied by decreased female fertility—a population could plummet, simply because too few people reached reproductive age to replace those dying of natural causes. Although mass deaths may well have occurred in some local areas, such catastrophes were not a necessary component of the Maya collapse.

The major archaeological projects that followed World War II provided additional details about events at the time of the collapse. Tikal again offers a typical case. Lower-class neighborhoods of the site were decimated during the collapse; the abundant house platforms of earlier times had been almost uni-

The small site of Jimbal, located north of Tikal, also began to erect stelae in the mid-ninth century. The ruler displayed on Jimbal Stela 1 does not use an emblem glyph in the inscription here, but uses the Tikal emblem glyph on a second stela at the site. The glyphs in square cartouches (shaded in light brown) and the floating figures surrounded by "blood scrolls" are features found in Terminal Classic carvings.

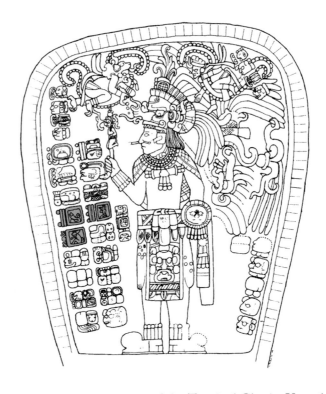

OVERLEAF: People still lived in the old stone palaces at Maya sites in the Terminal Classic, but they discarded their garbage in rooms and courtyards and neglected maintenance so that some buildings were already beginning to collapse. Although their pottery indicates that these late squatters were descendants of people who had lived at the same sites in better times, they were no longer able to maintain the traditions of earlier palace occupants.

formly abandoned by the beginning of the Terminal Classic. Yet, when Peter D. Harrison of the University of New Mexico excavated the stone palace structures of the Central Acropolis (the principal palace area just south of the Great Plaza), he and his team discovered a very different story. Almost all the palace buildings contained great piles of Terminal Classic refuse. But unlike the kings of yore, these later palace occupants were an untidy lot. Their garbage mounded up in the corners of rooms or was tossed out the doorways into once-immaculate courtyards. Maintenance was neglected and, in a few cases, the stone roofs collapsed while people still lived in the old buildings; the occupants simply shoved the debris into corners and continued living in those sections where the roof was still intact. Later excavations of other palace buildings, even those in rural areas, found evidence of the same kind of careless occupants. It points to the fact that, during the Terminal Classic, the stone palace was occupied by squatters; once the former occupants were no longer there, others used the stone buildings for shelter. But who were these squatters? From every indication, they were not a new population from elsewhere, but the descendants of the people who had lived at Tikal for generations. Their pottery was a clear outgrowth of earlier traditions; it had lost little in technical expertise, and for practical purposes was as well made as pottery at the height of the Classic. But gone was the hand-painted decoration that had marked the pottery of more prosperous times.

This vessel came from the last major tomb in the center of Tikal, which was placed in a building that was never finished. Whether the tomb might be that of one of the last rulers of the site is not clear. The simple, bichrome design on this vessel was also found on pieces in two other eighth-century burials.

Despite the squalor of the palace compounds, the temples and ceremonial plazas remained sacred places. Few new stelae were carved during the Terminal Classic. Instead, old stelae were hauled hither and yon across sites and set up in new locations. At Tikal, two-fifths of the stelae that archaeologists discovered in the Great Plaza had been re-erected there in Terminal Classic times. But they were set up in disregard for the old sacred formulae. In Classic times, stelae were usually placed in sets that corresponded to the sacred numbers of the Maya—seven, nine, thirteen—numbers that called down good fortune from the gods. The Terminal Classic Maya, on the other hand, thought nothing of adding another stela to a set, leaving, for example, eight stelae in a row—an unhappy number that could hardly have pleased the gods. During these times, the upper half of an uncarved stela was moved from the West Plaza at Tikal and set up in the Great Plaza, where it was paired with an altar fashioned from a fragment of an ancient carved stela.

The same neglect of propriety is evident in cached offerings. In the full Classic, offering rituals were very precise; one can imagine learned masters of ceremonies consulting ancient books and planning the rituals with an attention to tradition and protocol equal to that governing the inauguration of the British monarch or the installation of a new Pope. When a stela was erected, for example, a carefully prescribed set of objects was placed underneath it. The objects invariably included nine pieces of obsidian on which were incised the heads of gods, as well as nine oddly shaped "eccentric flints" (but never eccentric obsidians, which were reserved for other kinds of caches). At the outset of the construction of a new building or the remodeling of an old one, a different—but no less strictly prescribed—set of objects was placed in standard locations underneath the floors. The Terminal Classic Maya, on the other hand, sometimes neglected caches altogether; on other occasions they made such offerings, but did them wrongly, perhaps placing objects they had encountered somewhere in a building cache under a reset stela. In one instance, they broke into an important Early Classic burial site high on the North Acropolis at Tikal, perhaps to rob jades. When they refilled the pit they had created, they dumped in eccentric flints and incised obsidians pillaged from a Late Classic stela cache.

One can only speculate about the reason behind these aberrant ceremonies. Did someone, perhaps, still claim descent from the old kings, and thus celebrate their memory by resetting their monuments? Or did some barbarian chief, risen to leadership from the ranks of the peasants, harken back to now-fading tales of ancient splendor and demand his own stela, although no specialist survived to write the new ruler's name or inscribe his deeds? Another possibility is that the books that described the ceremonies might well have been lost in the general disruption of Maya society. Maybe the books were still treasured, but no one remained to decipher the mystic—now magical—markings that filled their pages. The ancient knowledge had perished, except for a vague idea that it was done "something like this."

The collapse, of course, did not occur at exactly the same time everywhere. At Tikal, no new construction was undertaken during the Terminal Classic, but at nearby Uaxactun, several large Terminal Classic palaces were erected before the collapse decimated the site and squatters overran the newly finished palaces. The situation in the Pasion River zone was even more mixed. Dos Pilas and Aguateca were abandoned early—even before the Terminal Classic started; on the river, meanwhile, population actually increased during the Terminal Classic at both Altar de Sacrificios and Seibal. At Seibal, the population increase was accompanied by a burst of construction and stela dedication. The major architectural groups were refurbished, while a new temple with four stairways—each with a stela placed at its foot—was erected in the central plaza. Seibal was flourishing, but perhaps under the leadership of a new elite. The Terminal Classic stelae there show a number of unusual features that depart from traditional Classic standards, and the individuals they portray would have looked very strange to the eyes of a good Classic Maya: Waist-length hair flows down their backs, and their noses are pierced and adorned with bones. The glyphs at Seibal also show unusual features. Many are enclosed within square cartouches, and some of the names are of a calendar style resembling that used by the Mexicans and people to the north. It seems likely that these non-Classic features of the late Seibal carvings derive in some manner from the northern Maya area in Yucatan. But the florescence along the Pasion was brief. Within a century or so the new programs of construction and stela building slowed, then ceased, leaving both Seibal and Altar de Sacrificios subject to the same decline as other sites.

EXPLAINING THE COLLAPSE

What had happened to the Classic Maya? The question began to be asked as soon as the inscriptions' sudden end became clear in the early part of this century. It continues to be asked today, usually attached to some phrase such as "the mysterious end of Maya civilization." I refuse to accept the term "mystery" as any longer applicable; we do not know all the details of the Maya collapse, and probably never will, but we *do* know why the Maya could not have continued living as they did during the Late Classic.

Early explanations of the Maya collapse ran the gamut of potential calamities, mostly of a sudden and catastrophic nature. Scientists invoked such natural disasters as epidemic disease, climatic change, and failure of the agricultural system, as well as social disruptions such as invasion by outsiders, war between Maya sites, or rebellion of the peasant masses. Most of these suggestions are not in themselves unreasonable, and many of them are still included as possible factors in modern discussions of the collapse. But one fundamental error of early archaeologists was the assumption that Classic Maya culture had been well adjusted and stable to begin with. Up until the mid-point of this century, that assumption was not illogical. The inscriptions, then the primary source of infor-

The Terminal Classic carving at Seibal departed significantly from earlier traditions. This stela, showing a monkey-masked individual, lacks the frame that usually outlined carvings and has no hieroglyphic text. The carving also is poorly done.

mation about change over time, showed little change for 600 years except for occasional adjustments of calendrical niceties. There was almost no information about population, and most Early Classic structures were buried, so that little could be said about their kind or number. The Maya did, indeed, look like a stable society, and it was reasonable to expect that they should have continued so unless overwhelmed by some sudden catastrophe.

Perhaps the most important revelation of Maya research in the last 40 years has been to show that Maya culture was neither unchanging nor stable. Population figures show an ever-escalating upward curve, as do the numbers of sites and major constructions. By the Late Classic, the Maya had surpassed all their previous achievements in a variety of ways. The future was filled with new challenges, but past successes were no guarantee that they would face the new challenges with equal success.

The key change in archaeological thinking about the Maya collapse is a recognition that the society was under prodigious stress. If one looks past the glory and the glitter of the Late Classic—past the great kings and their haughty proclamations—one sees multiple stressors: population growth and the agricultural adaptation it necessitated; a burgeoning elite segment; heightened competition between sites, perhaps associated with greater frequency and furor of war; pressures—both economic and military—from neighbors in Yucatan. Even though we still cannot pinpoint the precise cause of the failure, it is clear that in the Late Classic the Maya had reached a point of societal expansion that was exceedingly difficult to control; the culture simply had inadequate capabilities to face a growing number of problems.

The proud ruler Ah Bolon Tun of Seibal revived the site briefly in the Terminal Classic and in A.D. 849 dedicated five stelae that bear his portrait. Unlike earlier Maya rulers, he has shoulder-length hair, a mustache, and an ornament that pierces the left side of his nose. Most archaeologists believe that he was an outsider from the northern part of the lowlands.

The study of skeletons can provide information about the health and nutritional status of ancient populations. In this photo, archaeologists Richard E.W. Adams *(left)* and the late A. Ledyard Smith *(right)* record a burial at the site of Altar de Sacrificios.

POPULATION AND SUBSISTENCE STRESS

If we project the curve of world population growth for the last few centuries into the future, the results are ridiculous. It is not that our figures and projections are incorrect; it is simply that a continuation of present growth over the next few hundred years would mean that the resulting population would not have room to stand on our planet, let alone feed itself. Ultimately, then, the upward curve of population growth must end—perhaps with great human suffering. The Maya in the Late Classic were, within their region, in much the same situation. Their population had grown exponentially for centuries; it had reached the nearly unbelievable overall density of more than 500 people per square mile (200 per square kilometer), among the highest densities in the world. Such growth was bound to stop.

Because simple slash-and-burn farming could not hope to support such a gargantuan population, the Maya had turned to a variety of more intensive agricultural techniques, as discussed in Chapter 4. The new agricultural system walked a tightrope between success and disaster. Parts of it were new and untried; parts were at the statistical edge of failure—successful in good years, a total loss in bad. For a time, the Maya supported twice as many people as could be fed using simpler methods, but not without the risk of a growing dependence upon new systems—the long-range effects of which were unknown.

Although the high population density can be ascertained from archaeological evidence, there are no direct means to estimate quantities of food available in the past. There are, however, indications of nutritional stress in the skeletal material recovered from Maya sites. Adult stature declined in the Late Classic at both Tikal and Altar de Sacrificios, while anomalies in the bones and teeth at both these sites and Copan indicate nutritional deficiencies. This seems to me very important evidence; I can think of no other factor than nutritional stress that adequately explains a population loss of such magnitude.

SOCIOPOLITICAL STRESS

Socially, as well, the escalating intensity of Maya Classic civilization must have created stresses. As the art demonstrates over and over again, the elite were accustomed to privileges. The murals from Bonampak, for example, portray humbly costumed servants rushing hither and yon, dressing nobles in richly decorated clothing, and bedecking them with jewelry of imported shell and jade—the rarest of Maya valuables. As we have seen, the tombs of kings were stocked with riches: items imported from distant locations, the works of master painters of pottery and carvers of precious stone. And incessantly, gods and glory demanded ever-bigger structures. Temples soared upward and were constantly rebuilt, for the sake of even more grandeur. Palaces and carefully paved patios sheltered the rich among the Maya, while stone carvings celebrated their accomplishments. The enormous cost of such undertakings is obvious; in the final analysis, it was the bulk of the population—the peasant class—who bore the brunt of the expense, food, and labor. (Despite these burdens, however, the standard of living of Maya peasants seems to have been relatively high, and there are no indications of any reprisals against their lords. Few archaeologists today would argue that peasant rebellions were at the heart of the Maya collapse.)

For the elite, the political situation must have become increasingly unstable in Late Classic times. We have already discussed the hints of such instability in inscriptions. Kings within sites were forced to spread privileges among the lesser nobility in a perhaps desperate attempt to maintain a semblance of control. On a grander scale, the satellites that had previously been tightly bound to larger sites were now following their own agendas, failing to deliver the tribute needed to support the centers, and usurping prerogatives that had previously belonged exclusively to their masters.

Throughout these changes, sites competed bitterly for many things—prestige, trade, subjects, probably often for territory—and one of the important mechanisms of this competition was warfare. The data from both epigraphy and archaeology suggest an escalation in warfare during the Late Classic. Many scholars also believe that there was a change in the nature, as well as

This section of the murals at Bonampak graphically portrays the life of the elite. Here a member of the privileged class is being fitted out in all his finery by a retinue of servants.

the intensity, of warfare. They envision early Maya war focusing primarily on the capture of prisoners for sacrifice, and suggest it had little impact on the general populace. As the stresses of the Classic period mounted, however, military objectives were increasingly the conquest of territory, making war more and more destructive to the common people. Such changes, striking at the heart of everyday life, obviously might have precipitated or hastened the disintegration of Classic Maya society, but any fundamental change in the nature of warfare is perhaps immaterial. Given the stresses of the Late Classic, an intensification of the existing patterns would itself have proved sufficiently destructive.

There may also have been conflict with the Maya from the northern lowlands. It is clear that some of them came to sites such as Seibal during the Terminal Classic; what is not clear is whether they came to exploit an already weakened south or were, instead, a major cause of that weakness.

LESSONS FROM THE PAST
The most lucid conclusion of this discussion is that in the eighth century Maya Classic culture simply came apart. It came apart not because of a specific event,

but because it had reached a critical level of vulnerability: Incidents that might have caused little disruption in more stable times could now touch off an ineluctable downward spiral. We may never know either the initial nature, or the exact sequence, of those events that precipitated the Maya collapse. It would be satisfying to know such things, but it seems to me more important to understand how such events fit into a context in which disaster was likely—a context in which centuries of growth, and adaptation to growth, had created a situation that proved, in the long run, unsupportable.

There is, I believe, a sobering lesson in the collapse of Classic Maya civilization. The curve of Maya population growth was exponential, a kind of growth that provides less and less reaction time as numbers escalate. The Maya reacted to this growth through a variety of ecological and social adaptations—measures which led to their downfall. In agriculture, for example, they may have reaped advantageous short-term results at the expense of disastrous long-term consequences. Food supply increased, feeding population growth, which remained very high for a couple of centuries. But untried, perhaps desperate, measures to increase production can have unforeseen long-term consequences. The damage from slow processes such as erosion or salt-buildup in soils can accumulate gradually, until suddenly agricultural production plummets. The long-term consequences may be unanticipated and unintended, but they are nonetheless inherent in achieving the desired short-term results. Similarly, short-term social expedients such as extending elite privileges to a wider and wider group, or shifting the emphasis in warfare to focus upon conquest, may ultimately have proved maladaptive.

In the modern world, the curve of population growth over the last several centuries has also been exponential—a fact that can hardly have escaped the attention of any educated individual. In addition, the industrial world has, in recent centuries, achieved remarkable success in productivity, thus substantially raising the standard of living of a significant segment of the world's population. These positive short-term results have been based upon a lavish use of fossil fuels, the long-term consequences of which we are only now beginning to grasp. The supply of fossil fuels will soon be exhausted; yet the groups involved in their production are so powerful that only minimal effort has been made to develop alternatives. Meanwhile, the carbon dioxide released from fossil fuels threatens—in fact, the process has already begun—a greenhouse effect. Other natural resources are being ravished, with potentially devastating results: The alarming rate at which rain forests are being cleared, for example, spells disastrous consequences for world climates and the oxygen supply. At the same time, cracks are appearing in the social structures of the industrial world. Whole economic systems crumble overnight; corruption is rife, seemingly beyond control; ancient ethnic antagonisms erupt once more into slaughter. Do we face a future calamity akin to the Maya collapse? At the very least, we must face that possibility and ask whether our own system is spinning rapidly out of control.

A small Postclassic town built on the Caribbean coast of the Yucatan, Tulum was surrounded by a defensive wall. The Castillo, the main then, is a landmark along the coast. Tulum was a trading center for seafaring Maya merchants and probably still was occupied at the

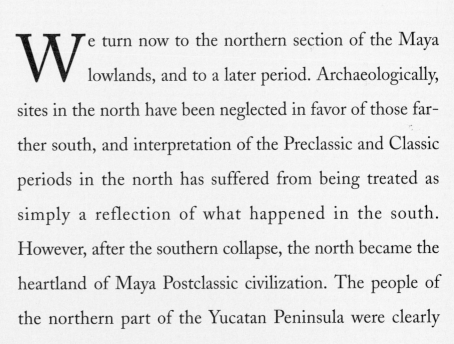

8

THE POSTCLASSIC MAYA

We turn now to the northern section of the Maya lowlands, and to a later period. Archaeologically, sites in the north have been neglected in favor of those farther south, and interpretation of the Preclassic and Classic periods in the north has suffered from being treated as simply a reflection of what happened in the south. However, after the southern collapse, the north became the heartland of Maya Postclassic civilization. The people of the northern part of the Yucatan Peninsula were clearly

pyramid, overlooks the ocean and now, as time of the Spanish conquest.

Maya; also clear is the fact that they interacted with the Maya of the southern lowlands. But cultural expression in the north was always somewhat different; the style of architecture and ceramics was distinct, for example, while the use of stone carvings and inscriptions never took root in the north to the same degree as in the south. Archaeologist David Freidel maintains that this difference reflects a different society. The people of the north, he believes, were never prey to the obsession with royal bloodlines that permeated southern culture; their more open society was, by the time of the Postclassic, more adaptive than that of the rigid south.

THE PUUC SITES

The Puuc area is a hilly region located somewhat inland from the western coast of Yucatan. Five large sites—Uxmal, Kabah, Labna, Sayil, and Oxkintok—as well as many medium and smaller sites, are crammed into the

The Great Palace at Sayil, one of the major Puuc sites, expanded during the 150 years after its founding to three stories containing almost 100 rooms. Sayil exhibits the open spaces and clean lines of the Puuc style.

Puuc architects and builders were masters of the corbeled arch and used it to great dramatic effect. This arch, which connects two courtyards at the site of Labna, is one of the most beautiful examples. The upper facades of the small side buildings show typical Puuc embellishments.

hill country, a small, roughly circular area of about 60 miles (97 kilometers) in diameter. In a recent archaeological project at Sayil, the University of Pittsburgh's Jeremy A. Sabloff—the general editor of this series—and his colleagues showed that the site had about 10,000 residents in its central area and another 7000 in the peripheries; the other Puuc sites are probably of comparable or even larger size. This unusual conjugation of sites seems to have been short-lived, and to have lasted only for a few centuries between A.D. 700 or 800 and A.D. 1000. In other words, the Puuc sites are not really Postclassic in time: they overlapped the Late and Terminal Classic periods in the south. They represent a full, although rather different, expression of Classic Maya culture.

A visitor accustomed to the southern Classic sites is struck by the spaciousness of Puuc sites. Plazas are designed on a larger scale, and the eye is greeted by long-distance vistas that southern sites lack. Another instant impression is that the lines of Puuc architecture are somehow cleaner. Walls seem straight

The stately Palace of the Governor at Uxmal is considered by many to be the most perfect Maya lowlands building. Behind it in the distance stands the Pyramid of the Magician, the only major temple-pyramid at the site.

and square, lacking the embellishments with which southern architects played with light and shadow. Straight and unadorned lower walls give way above doorways to tall upper facades decorated in geometrically patterned stone mosaics. Rounded columns and half columns are used, sometimes to frame doorways, but more often to give a fluted effect to an entire exterior wall or an upper facade. Puuc architects used the Maya arch to stunning effect. The arch through which one exits a building complex, for example, may frame an important building in the distance; at Kabah, a freestanding arch without attached building affords a stunning view of what was once the causeway leading to Uxmal.

The particular kinds of buildings and their arrangement in Puuc sites also distinguishes them from southern sites. The tall temple-pyramids that dominate southern sites are far less common in the Puuc; instead, the focus is on long, low buildings with multiple doorways, all arranged around spacious

courtyards. Appearing to Spanish eyes like convents or monasteries (hence the name "Nunnery Quadrangle" for the major complex at Uxmal), these groups more likely served the same elite residential and administrative functions as did southern palaces.

The characteristic construction style of the Puuc is most evident wherever the cross section of a wall has been exposed by collapse. Departing from the earlier method of one large block piled upon another, a section of Puuc masonry reveals a concrete core veneered with a facing of thin stones, each cut in such a way that a "boot" projects into the concrete interior.

The most famous Puuc site is Uxmal. Fifty miles (80 kilometers) south of Merida in a flat area that belies the hilly character of most of the Puuc, Uxmal's rosy-hued buildings stand out against the surrounding low scrub forest. The tallest structure is the pyramid called the Adivino—or Pyramid of the Magician. Like a southern temple-pyramid, it towers above the rest of the site;

yet despite its commanding height (or perhaps because of it), the Adivino seems somehow awkward and out of place. Pushed into a corner, away from the heart of the site, it is too close to the striking Nunnery Quadrangle to be visually effective. The Nunnery Quadrangle itself is neither out of place nor ineffective: its geometry catches the eye from any vantage point in the building groups to the south. The view through the nunnery's southern arch is dominated by the stately House of the Governor; considered by many the most perfect single building in the Maya lowlands, it is an architectural masterpiece of a very formal style. The building is an imposing 340 feet (104 meters) long, with a giant terrace that towers some 50 feet (15 meters) above neighboring plazas. Its facade once boasted stucco figures. Jeff Kowalski, specialist in Maya art and architecture from Northern Illinois University, suggests in his recent book *The House of the Governor: A Maya Palace at Uxmal, Yucatan, Mexico* (the most authoritative source on the building) that the figures were portraits of Uxmal's best-known ruler, Lord Chac. The few inscriptions at the site mostly deal with Lord Chac's reign in the late ninth and early 10th centuries, and he seems to have built most of the major structures, including the House of the Governor.

Styles of art and architecture at other Puuc sites are so strikingly similar to those at Uxmal that one cannot avoid the feeling they were very closely related—perhaps even under a single ruler. The sites seem also to have shared a common fate, for they were all abandoned at about the same time in the late 10th century. The reason for this secondary collapse—a century or so after that of the south—has not been studied in detail. While it may have been related to the political maneuverings of Chichen Itza, it may well have been precipitated by a period of enormously dense population that was doubtless difficult to support.

CHICHEN ITZA

Chichen Itza, perhaps the most-visited site in all the Maya area, lies some 75 miles (121 kilometers) east and slightly north of the Puuc zone. Located in the flat northern plains of Yucatan, the site offers a clear view to the horizon. In earlier days, when the surrounding land was stripped of trees, the largest buildings must have been visible for miles around.

Individual styles of architecture distinguish two sections of Chichen Itza. At the southern end of the site, the architecture is very similar to that of the Puuc region. Until recently, this section was called "Old Chichen" by archaeologists, its architectural style labeled "Pure Florescent." Buildings at the northern end, meanwhile, are remarkably different from those elsewhere in Maya country, showing foreign influences from somewhere to the north, in Mexico. This section of the site was first designated "Toltec Chichen" and the style "Modified Florescent." The traditional view among archaeologists was that the "Old Chichen" was indeed earlier, having its roots in a purely Maya tradition, and that the section known as "Toltec Chichen" was established when it was invad-

Chichen Itza's Temple of the Warriors and the long colonnaded hall associated with it have a mass of square columns that are carved with scenes of warriors and prisoners. The columns once supported wooden beams that roofed the structures, an architectural innovation that first appeared at Chichen Itza.

ed by Toltecs from Mexico. Unfortunately, uncomplicated interpretations in archaeology frequently turn out to be wrong; and so it was with the two Chichens. For a variety of reasons having to do with the niceties of ceramic chronology, it now seems that there was some kind of overlap—either partial or complete—in the time at which the two sections were in use.

The Toltec area of Chichen Itza contains the grander structures, dominated by the Castillo—a four-stairwayed pyramid rising in nine terraces, topped by a squat, flat-roofed temple. To one side, the Castillo overlooks the Great Ball Court, the largest court known from the Maya area, with a playing alley about 165 yards (150 meters) in length. Carvings on the side walls of the ball court display grisly scenes, in one of which a decapitated ballplayer kneels while his neck gushes blood that metamorphoses into writhing snakes. To the other side, the Castillo looks down upon a group of structures including the Temple of the Warriors and the Market. A whole forest of columns—each carved with scenes depicting warriors and prisoners—once supported wooden beams that held up the roofs of these buildings, a new style of roof-making that allowed much more interior space than did the corbeled stone arches used earlier.

Both architecture and art show influences from central Mexico. The closest similarities are between Chichen Itza and the site of Tula, in the Mexican state of Hidalgo. Just north of Mexico City, Tula is nearly 700 miles (1127 kilome-

The chacmool figure reclines at the head of the stairs to the Temple of the Warriors. The figure, which may have served as a sacrificial altar, is identical to chacmools at the distant, non-Maya site of Tula, slightly north of Mexico City.

The feathered serpent—Kukulcan to the Maya, Quetzalcoatl to the Toltecs—figures in the legends and art of both cultures as both a god and a human ruler. The legends, however, are too vague to be used as history.

ters) from the Yucatan Peninsula. Between 950 and 1200, Tula was the home base of a substantial Toltec empire in central Mexico. The open colonnades and buildings whose roofs were supported by columns in the "Toltec" section of Chichen are almost exact duplicates of structures at Tula. Both sites use columns depicting feathered serpents with heads turned downward and tails pointed to the sky. Both sites also feature carvings of human skulls, jaguars, and eagles devouring human hearts, as well as reclining *chacmools* with depressions in their bellies (the ashtray-like potential of which has not escaped manufacturers of tourist trinkets). Added together, these common features are undeniable proof of contact between the Maya and central Mexican peoples.

The nature of that contact, however, is not so easy to determine. Legends from both central Mexico and the Maya area speak of a great leader, a man called Kukulcan in Maya and Quetzalcoatl in the language of the Toltecs (both names meaning "feathered serpent"). The Toltec legends say that Quetzalcoatl was a good and just leader who was tricked by an enemy into committing sins that brought disgrace upon him; forced to leave Tula, he journeyed to the gulf coast, where he either burned himself in a great sacrificial fire or sailed eastward into the ocean, promising to return. The Maya legends, meanwhile, report that a great foreign leader named Kukulcan arrived in Yucatan to establish himself as king. Related in this simple manner, the tales seem such a straightforward answer to the origin of Mexican influences at Chichen Itza

THE SACRED CENOTE

Undoubtedly the most famous sacrificial location in all of the Maya area is the Sacred Cenote—or Cenote of Sacrifice—at Chichen Itza. Three hundred yards (274 meters) north of the Castillo, to which it is connected by a wide causeway, the Cenote is a well 165 feet (50 meters) in diameter and 65 feet (20 meters) deep from its rim to the surface of the water. Long after Chichen Itza had ceased to be a major center, the Maya continued to make pilgrimages to the site and to add more sacrifices to the horde in the Cenote. In a famous incident in 1536 (a year in which the Spaniards had been temporarily thrown out of Yucatan), the entire royal entourage of the ruler of the Xiu family was slaughtered by enemies on the way to make an offering at the Cenote. Bishop Landa was among those who extolled the importance of the place:

> Into this well they have had...the custom of throwing men alive as a sacrifice to the gods, in times of drought, and they believed that they did not die though they never saw them again. They also threw into it a great many other things, like precious stones and things which they prized. And so if this country had possessed gold, it would be this well that would have the greater part of it, so great was the devotion which the Indians showed for it.

In addition to skeletal remains, the Sacred Cenote at Chichen Itza has yielded treasures in abundance, including carved jade, bone, shells, and golden objects.

With this inducement, it was inevitable that the fetid water of the Cenote would be plumbed by archaeologists. From 1904-08, Edward H. Thompson, a U.S. consul in Yucatan and amateur archaeologist who had purchased the entire site of Chichen Itza, dredged the Cenote to see what might be salvaged. The anticipated treasures were, indeed, hidden under the murky water. Included was gold in a variety of forms, including a cup and saucer, rings, and hammered and embossed sheets showing warriors and scenes of sacrifice. Those golden objects, which were produced by casting, had to have come from distant locations as far away as Colombia and Panama, for the Maya themselves never learned to do more than hammer gold. Copper bells—symbolic of the death god Yum Cimil—had been thrown into the cenote in abundance, and there were objects of carved jade and bone, shells, and dozens of cakes of incense.

Finally, there were the remains of sacrificial victims. It was Maya custom, according to the 16th-century accounts, to cast victims into the cenote at daybreak, then to lower ropes at noon to remove those who were still alive and ask them for prophecies. Legends that beautiful young women were usually selected for sacrifice are contradicted by the skeletal evidence: most skeletons were those of children, while, among adults, males outnumbered females.

This exquisite jade plaque was found when the cenote was dredged.

The Books of Chilam Balam were written in Yucatec Maya (but using Spanish script) by native priests who were attempting to preserve memories of the ancient history and culture of their ancestors, but who also were continuing to practice Maya ceremonies.

that it may be hard to understand why archaeologists do not believe them. Yet, if one explores the details of the legends, many problems arise. To begin with, the date of Quetzalcoatl's exile is far too late to have affected Chichen; in addition, it is hard to see how an exiled leader and a small band of followers could have conquered the populous Maya communities in Yucatan. All in all, the stories seem to be myth—perhaps a myth with a germ of historical fact, but not the whole story.

An understanding of the period must also account for the Itza, the people for whom Chichen Itza—"the Well of the Itza"—was named. The 16th-century Spanish Franciscan, Bishop Landa, tells us of the Itza, as do the Books of Chilam Balam—18th-century chronicles written in Yucatec Maya using European letters. The Books of Chilam Balam contain material that may originally have been copied from hieroglyphic manuscripts, but they have been so altered and scrambled by later copyists that they are next to useless as historical sources. These sources identify the Itza—as they do Kukulcan—as foreigners. The Maya themselves did not know how the Itza related to Kukulcan, for Landa reports that "they differ among themselves as to whether he arrived before or after the Itzas or with them." In the legends reported by Landa and the Books of Chilam Balam, the Itza had a less than shining image. They were referred to as "those who speak our language brokenly," described as "people without fathers or mothers," and reported as being given to idolatry and lascivious practices. Nevertheless, it was the Itza, with or without Kukulcan, who established themselves at Chichen Itza and were to rule the entire Yucatan Peninsula for two centuries. The modern consensus is that the Itza were probably a Maya-speaking group like the Chontal—or Putun—Maya of the Spanish-contact period, whose homeland was along the gulf coast of Mexico. The Gulf Coast Maya, whose dialect was quite different from Yucatec—the variety of Maya spoken on the peninsula—would naturally speak Yucatec brokenly; also, they had been in contact with non-Maya people from Mexico for generations. At the time of contact with the Spanish, the Chontal were traders and seafarers, as their ancestors probably were too. It is thought that in the Postclassic the Gulf Coast Maya gradually spread along the coast of the Yucatan Peninsula, then struck inland to Chichen Itza. Murals at Chichen Itza show two peoples with different uniforms engaged in bitter battles, suggesting that the entry of the Itza was probably not peaceful.

Even though the Itza arrival was militaristic, the outcome is no longer seen as a simple conquest after which Itza rulers lorded it over helpless locals. Instead, the intrusion generated a new hybrid culture that combined old Maya customs with new ideas—some of Mexican origin—introduced by the Itza. The site was ruled not by the Itza alone, but by a consortium of newcomers and members of the local elite. Unlike Classic times, when a single ruler prevailed, power was now exercised by a larger ruling body. This kind of coalition government is known to have held sway later at a site called Mayapan, and

Coba reached its peak of glory in the Classic period, but continued to be an important city until about A.D. 1100. Approximately 50,000 people lived in the metropolis.

Linda Schele and David Freidel consider it the secret of Chichen Itza's success. A cluster of Maya inscriptions at Chichen—dating to a 20-year interval around 870—seem to confirm new political institutions. Befitting the new order, the inscriptions do not focus on a single "king," but instead name a number of individuals who all participate in major ceremonies. The individuals refer to each other as brothers, and as many as two or three sets of brothers seem to be involved in governing.

Some time in the 10th or 11th century, the rulers of Chichen Itza moved to gain control of the peninsula. They may have attacked the Puuc centers, thus contributing to the sites' abandonment. Another major opponent of the Itza was Coba, an old city toward the east coast of Yucatan that had been important since Classic times. The layout and architectural designs of Coba are so like Classic centers in the south that it has always seemed a possible outpost of that area. Coba was long considered to have been active only during the Classic period, until the findings of a recent project confirmed its continued existence as a site until about 1100. During the period between 800 and 1000, the city seems to have been the center of a power sphere in eastern Yucatan, first as a counterpart to a western sphere centered in the Puuc, then as a roadblock to the expansive plans of Chichen Itza. But Chichen was to prevail, and Coba was abandoned. From the scarcity of other sites after 1100, Chichen Itza seems thenceforth to have held tight control of most of the peninsula. Not surprisingly, Chichen Itza did not survive for long. At around 1200 or

Mayapan is situated in the west central portion of the Yucatan peninsula and came into prominence after the fall of Chichen Itza. The colonnaded hall at the site is a typical type of structure that does not appear in Classic sites. The columns supported a beam roof, but there are no signs of walls dividing the interior into rooms.

1250, the site fell. Legends written down in Colonial times tell stories of intrigue, a seduced wife, an upstart ruler of a neighboring site, and the eventual military defeat of the Itza. The site was certainly abandoned, except for remnant populations living amid the already disintegrating structures, but it remained a sacred place to which the Maya made pilgrimages as late as the 16th century.

THE PERIOD OF MAYAPAN

Any power vacuum among the Maya was certain to be filled. After the collapse of Chichen Itza, it was the turn of Mayapan, out in the northern plains 30 miles (48 kilometers) southwest of Merida. By this time, the Maya had entered the Late Postclassic, generally considered to have lasted from 1250 until the arrival of the Spanish in the 1520s. Visually, Mayapan suffers by comparison with the stately buildings and striking vistas of earlier sites; its ceremonial heart is crowded into a tiny space. Its major structure, the Castillo, is modeled after the Castillo at Chichen Itza; but it is minuscule by comparison, crammed between other structures so that it draws little attention. George Andrews of the University of Oregon, in his study of Maya architecture, summarizes his impression of the site:

> [T]he main ceremonial center has become a mishmash of conflicting ideas of order, further obscured by an overlay of symbols and details borrowed from neighboring regions. Compared with the quiet dignity of Copan or the geometrical precision of Uxmal, the fragmentation and disorder of Mayapan is very pronounced.

Mayapan is a city seemingly thrown together at random. In its present state of decay, it is easy to forget that a fair number of the city's houses—especially at the center of the site—would have been rather elegant while they were intact and the walls still covered with plaster. Colonnaded halls—three solid walls, the fourth open save for a series of columns—are the distinguishing feature of Mayapan. The city's population was large and concentrated into a space that makes the site seem crowded: 3500 structures occur within 1.5 square miles (3.8 square kilometers). Unlike most earlier sites, the entire conglomeration is surrounded by a wall that defines an obvious border.

Chichen Itza had achieved a centralized authority in which a single site brought together control of the entire Yucatan Peninsula. Mayapan did the same, leaving behind more precise chronicles of how it was done. It was said that the ruler of Mayapan "invited" the lords of all the various provinces of Yucatan to reside permanently within his city, leaving major-domos in charge of their affairs at home; the lords were, in effect, held hostage at the center. The colonnaded halls that are such a characteristic trait of Mayapan may have been where the elite "guests" and their entourages lived.

The chronicles reveal that the various Maya provinces were ruled by a number of powerful families. Mayapan, for example, was run by the Cocom family, who portrayed themselves as having rescued the Maya from the tyranny of the Itza; but now it was their turn to play the tyrant. Antagonisms ran deep against the Cocom family, as well as between the ruling families of the various provinces. Bishop Landa describes the situation, using—as will be obvious—testimony from an informant of a rival family called Tutul Xiu.

> Among the successors of the house of Cocom was a very haughty man...and he made another league with the men of Tabasco, and he introduced more Mexicans into the city, and he began to play the tyrant and to make slaves of the poorer people. On this account the nobles joined with the party of Tutul Xiu, who was a just statesman like his ancestors, and they conspired to put Cocom to death. And this they did, killing at the same time all his sons, except one who was absent. They sacked his house and took away the lands which he had in cacao and in other fruits, saying that they paid themselves for what he had taken from them.

The fractiousness, anger, and vengeful spirit evident in the preceding statement were endemic among the families of the Yucatan; after the fall of

Mayapan, the peninsula dissolved into a series of tiny statelets headed by petty kings. Warfare and enmities were perpetual. By the time the Spanish arrived, Yucatan was divided into 19 provinces. Some were headed by an overall lord to whom the lords of provincial towns paid allegiance and whom they followed in war. Other provinces had only a council of town leaders called *batabs*, while still others were so divided that each town was an independent and cantankerous entity under its own batab. Although no single province seems to have been in the ascendant by the time of the conquest, one suspects that, had more time been allowed the Maya, a new leader eventually would have arisen to reunite Yucatan under a new center similar to Chichen Itza or Mayapan.

The foregoing treatment of the architecture and the political fragmentation of the Late Postclassic has been less than laudatory, and reflects the way in which the period has traditionally been viewed by archaeologists (it used to be called the Decadent Period). It seems only fair to introduce an alternative view espoused by a number of archaeologists who have been working with later sites. While they acknowledge the loss of some of the more spectacular elements of earlier Maya culture, their focus is on a change in values among the Maya. The Late Postclassic Maya were traders, pragmatists, men of the world.

The back wall of a Late Postclassic structure at San Gervasio, Cozumel, shows its rough stone masonry. Originally it was finished with a plaster coat. Cozumel contains almost no large or grand structures, but was a well-populated trade-oriented center with a famous oracle.

Francisco Hernández de Córdoba arrived in Yucatan in 1517 in search of slaves and gold, but met with heavy resistance from the Maya. He retreated to Cuba and died of his wounds there.

Keen on economic success, they saw little profit in the showy and spectacular, and were driven by what seems a very modern concern with the bottom line.

The island of Cozumel, off the east coast of Yucatan, typified this sort of trade-oriented attitude. The island contains almost no large structures, yet it had a substantial population. Given its fortuitous location, Cozumel was renowned as a trading center for coast-hugging canoes laden with merchandise. The island remained neutral in the midst of political turmoil, and welcomed all comers as long they had goods to trade. Cozumel was also home to a famous oracle, who spoke words of wisdom and was consulted by the Maya from throughout the peninsula—consulted, one suspects, for a price. In our own day, we are hardly in any position to denigrate a culture of profit-oriented businessmen, but those of us who have worked mostly in Classic sites find it hard not to do so. Perhaps we resent a certain loss of innocence (whether it was the Maya's innocence or our own is hard to say).

THE COMING OF THE SPANIARDS

When the first Spanish colonies—in the Caribbean islands—became crowded and strife-torn, bands of adventurers pushed on to new lands and new conquests. The first voyage to Yucatan was made by Francisco Hernández de Córdoba in 1517. Bernal Díaz, who would later chronicle Cortés' conquest of Mexico, describes Córdoba's departure: "We sailed at hazard towards that part of the horizon where the sun sets, utterly ignorant of shallows, currents, and the prevailing winds." Twenty-one days and a great storm later, they arrived off the coast of Yucatan; there they spied a town so impressive that they named it Gran Cairo. The Spaniards were conducted ashore by seemingly friendly natives—who promptly ambushed them. Still, they managed to carry off a number of wooden idols and a few trinkets of alloyed gold, enough to convince them that riches untold awaited in Yucatan. Juan de Grijalva soon followed Córdoba's lead and was also awed by what he saw:

> We followed the shore day and night, and the next day toward sunset we perceived a city or town so large, that Seville would not have seemed more considerable nor better; one saw there a very large tower; on the shore was a great throng of Indians, who bore two standards which they raised and lowered to signal us to approach them...

The Maya, however, proved stubborn: their subjugation was slow and halting. In 1527 and 1928 and again from 1531 to 1934, Spanish expeditions into Yucatan sputtered and were thrown back. The troubles were many. Movement was hindered and military tactics hampered by trackless jungle, swamps, and stony ground—all completely unsuitable for travel on horseback. Maya towns proffered friendship and swore fealty to the distant Spanish king, only to turn upon the Spaniards at the first opportunity that presented itself. Time and time again the Spanish commanders split their pitifully small forces to send

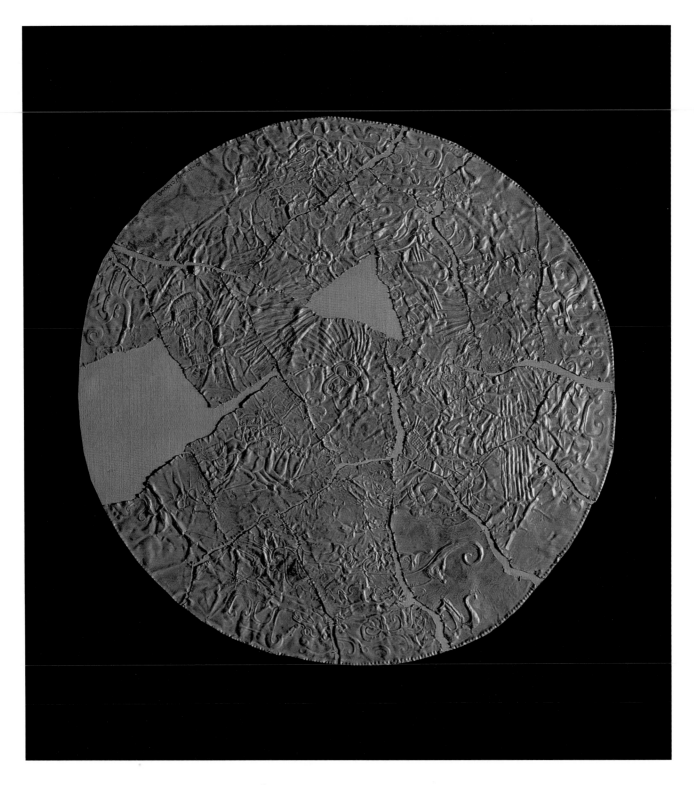

The battered fragments of an embossed gold disk from the cenote at Chichen Itza *(left)* depict the human sacrifice that so horrified the Spanish. In the illustration below, reconstructed from the original, the form of the ritual becomes more clear— extraction of the heart.

parties off in pursuit of the gold reported by the natives to lie to the east or to the west or just a little way ahead.

Attempts were made to found Spanish towns, but disease, hunger, and Maya spears took their toll; the towns dwindled and were abandoned. Discouragement was the greatest enemy. The men were fearless, a reckless lot hungry for frontier life, miles and months away from authority, living without rules or conventions. They accepted hardship as a matter of course, but they could not tolerate lack of reward. Lured into the wilderness by a dream of golden cities, they instead found limestone temples where blood-smeared priests offered the hearts of victims to the sky. Many drifted quietly away in disillusionment, despite threats of punishment for desertion.

Not until the mid-1540s would new campaigns and a new breed of settlers, satisfied with the simple rewards of land and Indian labor, finally establish a permanent Spanish presence. The town of Merida was established in 1542, and soon became the center of the growing Spanish colonies. The land was divided into haciendas for the Spanish colonists and the Indians who worked their land. European diseases—which had arrived with the first European contact—swept through the countryside in wave after wave, reducing Indian populations to a fragment of their original size. Most of Maya elite culture died very rapidly, although some hidden knowledge of writing and ceremonies probably persisted for as long as a century. The culture of the Maya peasantry, on the other hand, showed greater persistence; it was woven together with customs adopted from the Spanish to make a constantly changing and adapting culture that continues today.

THE MAYA OF TODAY

There are still more than four million people who speak Maya languages. Today's Maya occupy two large blocks of land, one running across the Yucatan Peninsula in the northern part of the lowlands, the second along the mountains that parallel the Pacific Ocean in Guatemala and the Mexican state of Chiapas.

It is in the highland villages of Chiapas and Guatemala that Maya culture survives in its most characteristic form. But it would be mistaken to believe that by visiting Maya villages one could look directly into a changeless past. Maya culture has been transforming itself for centuries—retaining some elements of the ancient past, adding dashes of Spanish colonial culture, then more recent ingredients, and stirring the mix into a blend that changes each year. I remember my first visit to the market at Chichicastenango in the Guatemalan highlands more than 30 years ago. There, amidst the handmade costumes and the incense fumes from ceremonies on the church steps, I suddenly realized with dismay that the strange chant floating over the scene from

The characteristic Maya culture still survives today in the highland villages of Guatemala and Mexico. More than four million people speak some form of Maya language.

loudspeakers was the music of Elvis Presley. It seemed a sacrilege at the time. But it was not; it was 1958 when I visited Chichicastenango, not 1458. To imagine that I was stepping into the past—simply because these people had ancient roots—was an illusion.

We have much to learn from the Maya of today, including some things that will help us better to understand the past. But today's Maya are not living fossils, like dinosaurs resurrected for an amusement park: they are a real people. True, they have a long history, they think and express their culture in a way truly their own. But, like us, they live in the 20th century; they have learned to fit their ways to contemporary realities because the only moment in which anyone can live is now.

Certainly, some aspects of the present-day Maya *are* old. One can still see faces that would be at home on stelae from Yaxchilan. Some highland villages still keep the old 365-day calendar with its 18 months of 20 days and its five

148

The market in Solola, Guatemala, is still mostly a Maya rather than a tourist market, but the products available are a mix of native and western goods.

unlucky days. People still tell the stories of a series of creations and destructions of the universe, resulting finally in the present universe because the gods at last had sense enough to fashion human beings out of maize dough. In Yucatecan ceremonies, small boys are still tied to the corners of a house and instructed to chirp like frogs; the participants call the boys "chacs," after the ancient rain god. Blood sacrifice still accompanies many ceremonies—but now a chicken is the usual victim—and it is easy to imagine that this is a vestige of ancient human sacrifice. Perhaps this is so, but the prayers now—although they may invoke the sun and moon—also call upon Jesus and Mary and a litany of saints who are certainly not from the Maya pantheon. The gods still appreciate the smoke of the ancient incense, but have also learned to enjoy offerings of distilled liquor and cigarettes fresh from the pack. In the highlands, most villages have a series of political and ritual offices for ambitious men, beginning with the responsibilities of sponsoring fiestas. The offices are passed from one holder to another with elaborate ceremonies that in some towns involve the exchange of ceremonial staffs; while the offices themselves were learned from the Spanish, the ceremonies must resemble the inauguration of the old kings.

Inevitably, change creeps on. The native costume in Yucatan is largely gone, except for the embroidered women's blouses and dresses; the embroidery, however, is now almost always done by machine rather than by hand. In the highland areas, both men's and women's costumes continue to be worn (albeit in a declining number of villages), but whereas textiles once were woven by women on backstrap looms, most are now made by men on a larger foot loom. When I was first in the highlands, a number of villages still made water jars by hand and marketed them to other centers that did not make pottery. Now, the market is full of gaudy plastic jugs painted in vibrant stripes of color, but of exactly the same shape as the handmade ones. Everybody uses them—after all, they are cheap, much lighter than pottery, and bounce harmlessly when dropped; no sensible person who had to carry water daily would ever use the beautifully handmade jars.

Yet Maya villages manage to retain their integrity as a separate culture, apart from the national culture surrounding them. Especially in the highlands of

Traditional costumes are still worn by modern Maya in the Guatemala highlands, though now they are more often than not woven on large foot looms rather than the old backstrap looms.

Many of the utilitarian objects once made from clay by the hands of Maya potters are now manufactured from lighter, more durable plastic or metal. Fortunately some of the old skills survive, as in these traditional water jars that are still being produced in a few pottery-making villages.

Guatemala, good land is still available, and villagers continue to farm corn, squash, and beans—sometimes using the old slash-and-burn methods. But in some places, carefully tended, irrigated gardens raise vegetables or flowers for the Guatemala City market and add to the villagers' meager income. Similarly, although many of the ancient crafts have died, the old techniques of pottery or textile-making are now turned to items that delight tourists (a more profitable market than anything existing 50 years ago).

The problems faced by the modern Maya are real. In much of the highlands, men migrate every year to the huge farms and coffee plantations near the Pacific Coast—where many fall prey to the dangers awaiting men far away from home. Whole families are deserting their villages at an alarming rate, joining the mass migration to the towns and cities in quest of possessions and opportunities that are lacking at home. Mostly, they find only the poverty and misery of the squalid barrios that house the urban poor. The Maya must face conflicting pressures from national and international culture. Some tell them to modernize and join the national economy; others, to perfect ancient sustainable agriculture. They are under pressure to desert their old ways, but are also instructed to retain their craft skills and preserve their costumes for the sake of the tourist industry. They are tormented by politicians—of both the left and the right—to fight wars and join movements that are not their own.

Whether or not Maya culture will survive is uncertain. As an anthropologist, I believe that something precious will be lost if it does not. But I am certain that the people will survive; that, after all, is what really counts.

REFERENCES

CHAPTER 1: SETTING THE STAGE

There are a number of general works on ancient Maya civilization that may be of interest to the reader who wishes to explore the topic in more detail. In preparing this book, I used the books of Hammond, Henderson, and Sharer. Sharer's revision of *The Ancient Maya* is particularly complete and useful as a reference source.

COE, MICHAEL D. 1987 *The Maya*. Thames and Hudson, London and New York.

GALLENKAMP, CHARLES 1987 *Maya: The Riddle and Rediscovery of a Lost Civilization*. Penguin Books.

HAMMOND, NORMAN 1982 *Ancient Maya Civilization*. Rutgers University Press and Cambridge University Press, New Brunswick and Cambridge, England.

HENDERSON, JOHN S. 1981 *The World of the Ancient Maya*. Cornell University Press, Ithaca.

SHARER, ROBERT J. 1983 *The Ancient Maya*. Fourth Edition, Revised. Stanford University Press, Stanford. (A descendant of previous editions by Sylvanus G. Morley and George W. Brainerd.)

CHAPTER 2: THE EARLY DAYS OF DISCOVERY

The works of Robert Brunhouse are an invaluable source for information about the archaeologists who have worked in the Maya area. Sabloff's volume is an excellent consideration of the changes that have taken place in Maya archaeology in recent years. The books of Stephens (although without the Catherwood illustrations) are still available in paperback editions. They and Tozzer's translation of Landa's manuscript are well worth reading. I also list the original edition of Thompson's volume and Morley's 1946 summary both of which are now mainly of historical interest.

BRUNHOUSE, ROBERT L. 1971 *Sylvanus G. Morley and the World of the Ancient Mayas*. University of Oklahoma Press, Norman.

1973 *In Search of the Maya: The First Archaeologists*. University of New Mexico Press, Albuquerque.

1975 *Pursuit of the Ancient Maya: Some Archaeologists of Yesterday*. University of New Mexico Press, Albuquerque.

MORLEY, SYLVANUS G. 1946 *The Ancient Maya*. Stanford University Press, Palo Alto.

SABLOFF, JEREMY A. 1990 *The New Archaeology and the Ancient Maya*. Scientific American Library, New York.

STEPHENS, JOHN L. 1841 *Incidents of Travel in Central America, Chiapas, and Yucatan*. two vols. Harper & Brothers, New York.

1843 *Incidents of Travel in Yucatan*. two vols. Harper & Brothers, New York. (Both in paperback editions from Dover Publications, New York.)

THOMPSON, J. ERIC S. 1954 *The Rise and Fall of Maya Civilization*. University of Oklahoma Press, Norman.

TOZZER, ALFRED M. 1941 *Landa's Relación de las Cosas de Yucatán: Translation*. Papers of the Peabody Museum of American Archaeology and Ethnology, vol. 18. Harvard University, Cambridge, Mass.

CHAPTER 3: THE GENESIS OF MAYA CIVILIZATION

Not much is available that deals directly with the Maya Preclassic. The Adams-edited book is the standard reference; the remainder deal specifically with particular sites.

ADAMS, RICHARD E. W. (EDITOR) 1977 *The Origins of Maya Civilization*. University of New Mexico Press, Albuquerque.

COE, WILLIAM R. AND JOHN J. MCGINN 1963 Tikal: the North Acropolis and an Early Tomb. *Expedition* 5(2):24-32.

DAHLIN, BRUCE H. 1984 A Colossus in Guatemala: the Preclassic Maya City of El Mirador. *Archaeology* 37(5):18-25.

MATHENY, RAY T. 1986 Investigations at El Mirador, Peten, Guatemala. *National Geographic Research Reports* 2(3):332-353.

MATHENY, RAY T. 1987 El Mirador: An Early Maya Metropolis Uncovered. *National Geographic* September: 317-339.

CHAPTER 4: THE CLASSIC IN FULL FLOWER

Andrews' volume is an excellent summary of Maya architecture, as well as having maps and good black-and-white photographs. It can serve as a guidebook for visiting sites, although it is rather large. Hunter's book is a more portable guide to carry into sites. Proskouriakoff's reconstruction drawings give an idea of what sites and structures looked like in their original condition. The Turner and Harrison volume was the breakthrough collection of professional articles describing the changed ideas about Maya agriculture.

ANDREWS, GEORGE F. 1975 *Maya Cities: Placemaking and Urbanization*. University of Oklahoma Press, Norman.

COE, WILLIAM R. 1988 *Tikal: A Handbook of the Ancient Maya*

Ruins. Second edition with revisions by Carlos Rudy Larios V. The University Museum, University of Pennsylvania, Philadelphia.

FERGUSON, WILLIAM M. AND JOHN Q. ROYCE 1977 *Maya Ruins of Mexico in Color.* University of Oklahoma Press, Norman.

HARRISON, PETER D. AND B. L. TURNER, II (EDITORS) 1978 *Pre-Hispanic Maya Agriculture.* University of New Mexico Press, Albuquerque.

HUNTER, C. BRUCE 1986 *A Guide to Ancient Maya Ruins.* University of Oklahoma Press, Norman.

PROSKOURIAKOFF, TATIANA 1976 *An Album of Maya Architecture.* University of Oklahoma Press, Norman. Reprint of 1946 publication.

CHAPTER 5: HIGH SOCIETY

Three books were key sources for me in preparing this chapter. Both Schele and Miller, and Schele and Freidel present the data from glyphic decipherment in a non-technical way, but replete with notes that supply detail on Maya history. The articles in *Classic Maya Political History* were also a valuable reference. Most importantly, the opportunity to interact with the authors of that volume educated me about glyphic decipherment. I also list Houston's brief summary of Maya hieroglyphic writing, and two of Proskouriakoff's articles, one her original contribution in 1960, the other a more readable summary for a general audience.

CULBERT, T. PATRICK (EDITOR) 1991 *Classic Maya Political History: Hieroglyphic and Archaeological Evidence.* Cambridge University Press, Cambridge, England.

HOUSTON, STEPHEN D. 1989 *Maya Glyphs.* British Museum Publications and University of California Press, London and Berkeley.

PROSKOURIAKOFF, TATIANA 1960 Historical Implications of a Pattern of Dates at Piedras Negras, Guatemala. *American Antiquity* 25:454-475. 1961 The Lords of the Maya Realm. *Expedition* 4(1):14-21.

SCHELE, LINDA AND DAVID FREIDEL 1990 *A Forest of Kings: The Untold Story of the Ancient Maya.* William Morrow and Company, New York.

SCHELE, LINDA, AND MARY ELLEN MILLER 1986 *The Blood of Kings: Dynasty and Ritual in Maya Art.* Kimbell Art Museum and George Braziller Inc., Fort Worth and New York.

CHAPTER 6: THE HISTORY OF THE CLASSIC MAYA

The references cited in the last chapter by Schele and Miller, Schele and Freidel, and the articles in my *Classic Maya Political History* were the key sources for this chapter as well. The additional items listed here supply information about individual sites or regions. Fash's book on Copan does a splendid job of integrating the archaeological and inscriptional evidence for a general audience.

FASH, WILLIAM L. 1991 *Scribes, Warriors and Kings: The City of Copán and the Ancient Maya.* Thames and Hudson, New York and London.

HOUSTON, STEPHEN D., AND PETER MATHEWS 1985 *The Dynastic Sequence of Dos Pilas, Guatemala.* San Francisco, Pre-Columbian Art Research Institute, Monograph 1.

JONES, CHRISTOPHER 1991 Cycles of Growth at Tikal. In *Classic Maya Political History: Hieroglyphic and Archaeological Evidence,* edited by T. Patrick Culbert, pp. 102-127. Cambridge University Press, Cambridge, England.

CHAPTER 7: THE COLLAPSE OF THE CLASSIC

The 1973 volume that I edited marks the beginning of the modern treatments of the Maya collapse. The other two articles look at the problem from more recent viewpoints.

CULBERT, T. PATRICK (EDITOR) 1973 *The Classic Maya Collapse.* University of New Mexico Press, Albuquerque.

RICE, DON S. AND PRUDENCE M. RICE 1984 Lessons from the Maya. *Latin American Research Review* 19(3):7-34.

SABLOFF, JEREMY A. 1993 Interpreting the Collapse of Classic Maya Civilization: A Case Study of Changing Archaeological Perspectives. In *Metaarchaeology,* edited by L. Embree. Kluwer Academic Publishers, Netherlands.

CHAPTER 8: THE POSTCLASSIC MAYA

The Chase and Rice, and Sabloff and Andrews volumes are the standard reference works on the Maya Postclassic and served as major sources for this chapter.

CHASE, ARLEN F. AND PRUDENCE M. RICE (EDITORS) 1985 *The Lowland Maya Postclassic.* University of Texas Press, Austin.

SABLOFF, JEREMY A., AND E. WYLLYS ANDREWS V (EDITORS) 1986 *Late Lowland Maya Civilization: Classic to Postclassic.* University of New Mexico Press, Albuquerque.

INDEX

PICTURE CREDITS

AUTHOR'S ACKNOWLEDGMENTS

As I have already said in the early pages of this book, this is an exciting time to be a Mayanist and to write about the Maya for a general audience. Things are changing so rapidly in Maya studies that learning is an unending process. The people from whom I have learned over the last 35 years are legion. I owe all of them a debt of gratitude, even though they are far too numerous to mention individually.

I must, however, make special note of all of my coworkers and friends of the Tikal Project with whom I shared ideas for years and who were crucial in helping me form my first concepts of the Maya. Thanks are owed as well to my colleagues from later years, especially those with whom I interacted in seminars at the School of American Research in Santa Fe. And, like any teacher, I have learned more from my students than I have taught them. I thank all of you.

In the preparation of this book, series editor Jerry Sabloff has been a source of encouragement, advice, and information. I am grateful to Patricia Gallagher and the editors at the Smithsonian Books for their confidence in asking me to write the book. All of the people with whom I worked at St. Remy Press, especially Carolyn Jackson as head of the editorial team, Chantal Bilodeau who designed the book, and Chris Jackson who secured the wonderful photographs, were gracious and patient and worked with enormous diligence.

Above all, I must give thanks to my wife, Bobbi Culbert, who kindly pointed out sections of the first draft that were beyond the ken of ordinary mortals (i.e., unintelligible), who helped locate some of the best illustrations, and who has—best of all—managed to put up with me for all these years.

How true it is that "no man is an island." Our work is always the result of contact with others. To all of you, named and unnamed, I give thanks.

T. Patrick Culbert,
Tucson, Arizona